S0-AER-911

The LOST HAMPTONS

The glorious 4th for the
honorable 5th.

For our Dick,
    who has revealed the manifold beauties
    and pleasures still extant in
    this charmed place.

        With love on his birthday
        from

            Michelle & Barrymore

Copyright © 2004 Steven Petrow
ISBN 0-7385-1187-0

First published 2004

Published by Arcadia Publishing,
an imprint of Tempus Publishing Inc.
Portsmouth NH, Charleston SC,
Chicago, San Francisco

Printed in Great Britain

Library of Congress Catalog Card Number: 2003101272

For all general information, contact Arcadia Publishing:
Telephone 843-853-2070
Fax 843-853-0044
E-mail sales@arcadiapublishing.com

For customer service and orders:
Toll-free 1-888-313-2665

Visit us on the Internet at www.arcadiapublishing.com

BEFORE THE STORM—AT SOUTHAMPTON, c. 1910. Talk of bringing the railroad to the Hamptons in the 1870s stirred up the locals. One critic said, "It is to be hoped that no large hotels and no very costly country places will ever be built in [East Hampton]." (Eric Woodward Collection.)

The LOST HAMPTONS

STEVEN PETROW

with Richard Barons

ARCADIA

Images in this book are from the following:

Eric Woodward Collection

Southampton Historical Museum

Harvey Ginsberg Postcard Collection

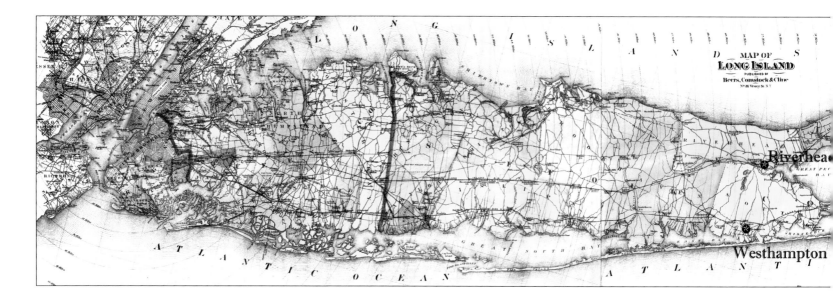

CONTENTS

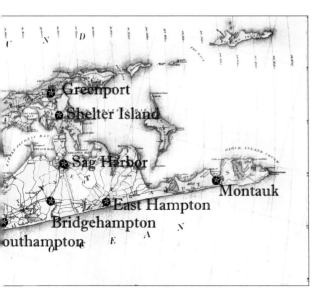

MAP OF LONG ISLAND'S EAST END, C. 1890.
(Southampton Historical Museum.)

For Laura Ann—always.

Maidstone Club, The Pool   East Hampton, Long Island, N. Y.

MAIDSTONE CLUB, THE POOL, EAST HAMPTON, C. 1930. Founded in 1891, the Maidstone Club quickly became the social hub of East Hampton. The saying of the time was "If you aren't in the Maidstone, you're out of it" (Eric Woodward Collection.)

THE HAMPTONS

Lost and Found

To the world at large, "the Hamptons" is an umbrella term like "the Riviera" or "the Catskills" or "the Islands" that describes a generic destination. To those of us who live on Long Island's South Fork, it is a convenient but meaningless catchall. We know that each of our towns, villages, and hamlets has its own distinctive character. They also have much in common, and there is no doubt that our history, as well as our contemporary life, reflects an undeniable regional identity. So, just in case any of us come down with Hamptonitis (blurred vision induced by exposure to glossy magazines and television programs that use the area as a backdrop for celebrity shenanigans), our weekly newspapers provide the antidote.

In addition to covering current events and reporting on each community's present-day concerns, several of the papers regularly run items that remind us of the past. Snippets of news columns from 50 or even 100 years ago—the *Southampton Press*'s "From Past Presses" and the *East Hampton Star*'s "The Way It Was," for example—testify that many of today's problems such as traffic, overdevelopment, beach erosion, and tension between summer and full-time residents have been with us for at least as long as the papers have been in business. Just as often, these items show how much things have changed. For example, I remember one article that described an automobile losing its brakes on an East Hampton hill and careening into Town Pond, an accident that could not happen today because the hill in question was leveled many years ago.

Even more evocative than such descriptions are the photographs and postcards culled from the papers' archives or sent in by readers that show us the places and people of bygone days. One venerable weekly, the *Sag Harbor Express* (first published in 1859), juxtaposes old pictures with shots of the same locales today—comparisons that give pause to newcomers and natives alike. They reinforce the longing for the good old days that furnishes Steven Petrow and Richard Barons with the raison d'être for this delightful book.

Nostalgia, it turns out, is relative. Let's face it: change is not always for the worse. Those who bewail the advent of tourism via automobile and airplane tend to wax poetic over the steam trains and side-wheelers, whose drawbacks are colorfully described in *The Lost Hamptons*. Graded and paved roads are clear improvements over the rutted, muddy tracks lamented in many editorials, and no one mourns the demise of the turnpike tollbooths. Would we really want to depend on a horse-drawn sleigh, however charming, to deliver the milk in winter, or spend the summer traveling to the beach in a jolting buckboard? And find me a 21st-century cook who would willingly cater a dinner party using the iron kettles and roasting spits in a picturesque 18th-century open hearth.

With these glimpses of a past we sometimes long to recapture, but in which we might not be especially comfortable or even welcome, the authors reveal the special qualities of the communities that fall under the Hamptons rubric. They also offer an engaging study of the collective history that has brought us to where we find ourselves today.

—Helen A. Harrison
Sag Harbor, New York
January 2003

The Riding Class, Southampton, L. I.

THE RIDING CLASS, SOUTHAMPTON, C. 1910. "Newport, Rhode Island, is a summer resort to which thousands of the wealthy throng each year to strive for social recognition. Southampton, Long Island, is a quiet seaside village where a few hundred of the old New York aristocracy go each summer to get away from Newport and all it signifies. Newport is rich and blatantly proud of it. Southampton is wealthy and gives the matter little concern." —Mrs. John King Van Rensselaer, Southampton summer colonist, 1924. (Eric Woodward Collection.)

INTRODUCTION

In researching this book, I have been asked incessantly, "What, another book about the Hamptons?" quickly followed by, "What did you learn?" Such is the mystique of the Hamptons, much written about but still the subject of endless curiosity, including mine.

Of course, I have read any number of books about the East End of Long Island—some good, some bad, most plain dreadful—but I thought there was something still unsaid. I found myself looking for that story, a Californian, arriving at the doorstep of the august East Hampton Library with a laptop, cell phone, and decaf latte in hand. Ducking into the Pennypacker Long Island Collection, the library's "fireproof" rare book room, I spiraled out of the 21st century, greeted by an antiquated card catalog (with its own *very* unique take on the Dewey decimal system), a "no pen" dictum, and a bevy of other rules and regulations said to protect the books but meant, perhaps, to intimidate newcomers.

Although I have lived in California for two decades, it was not as if I were a complete stranger to the East End community. My family has owned property in Southampton for nearly a half-century, but the Petrow house stands "north of the highway" in a district known as North Sea and humorously to early in the last century as the "Dead Sea." I had even been a junior tennis champion on the public courts of the old-time village in the early 1970s and had earned a handful of mentions of my comings and goings in the "Beachcomber" column of the *Southampton Press*, but even this recognition occurred only because the publisher of the *Press* had sold my parents their house.

Still, the venerable librarian Dorothy King, whose family first came to the East End in the late 1600s, seemed at first impervious to my comparatively shallow roots. For weeks I was lost, searching for my muse in musty boxes and dusty books. On my best behavior, I complied in calling her Miss King, while she firmly, albeit kindly, kept me mindful of the rules: no cell phones, no water, and, of course, no pens!

On one of those particularly muddied days, I perused *East Hampton History*, a thick volume with an exhaustive and exclusive genealogy, by Jeannette Edwards Rattray, East Hampton's unofficial town historian during the 1950s. I took copious notes about the difficulty outsiders faced in breaking into the town's tight-knit social fabric. "Clannish," "stubborn," and "hesitant to change" were some of Jeannette Rattray's favorite terms to characterize the town's favorite sons. Describing one prominent local family, she recounted, indeed rejoiced, "The Lesters have been in East Hampton *only* about two hundred years." With that news, I thought I might never get the insider's access and the fresh angle on the Hamptons for which I hoped.

Then one day Miss King asked me to call her "Dorothy" and inquired, "Would you like to see the picture postcards that were donated to the library last year?" "Have you shown them to a lot of other people?" the journalist in me replied. "Not really," she answered. Not only was I thrilled to have Miss King lower her guard, but the postcards delivered a riveting visual narrative of this quaint and picturesque town. Even better, most of the hand-tinted postcards had been secreted away for decades, as were those to be discovered later at the Southampton Historical Museum and in the even vaster collection of architect Edward Woodward.

These postcards portray the quiet villages, historic homes, and privet-lined lanes of the East End as early as the 17th century (although the cards themselves are of a much more recent invention). They depict life in the Hamptons as we have not seen it before. Stunning in their color, detail, and composition, the cards, originally photographs, illustrate a place and a way of life that have been lost—*The Lost Hamptons,* if you will. Filled with the high drama of celebrity, the glorious architecture of the time, and the quiet splendor of the East End's landscapes and seascapes, these photographs allow us to experience a world all but swallowed by time.

But, thanks to Miss King (I mean Dorothy—change comes slowly), I had my story and my book. During those seasons I spent burrowed in the library, the local papers—from *Dan's Paper,* an idiosyncratic weekly, to a glossy magazine called simply *Hamptons* (a term most locals detest because it blankets over the distinct qualities that make each of the villages special and different)—warned of the explosion of McMansions perched atop fragile dunes and the leveling of the few remaining potato fields. The historian in me could not help but chuckle. The more I read, the closer I understood the parallels between then and now. Debates about clean water, the overcrowding of roads, backed-up parking lots, even oversized houses and oversized egos, were as common yesterday as they are today.

Among year-rounders, a pervasive sentiment could be heard time and again: the summer people are ruining everything. Of course, the distinction between "summer colonists," as the first weekenders were known in the 19th century, and locals, or year-rounders, has become all but meaningless. Not too long ago, one paper added its two cents to the debate: "[T]he newcomer is anyone who came after you did, the native anyone who came before; the difference can be as little as a few years."

In the end what I found was that, for better and for worse, our generation, like every one that preceded it, sees only in the present tense. In truth, the Hamptons have been pronounced lost by every generation that has lived here, only to be found again by each subsequent generation. Such is the Hamptons' legacy to us. It may be convenient to blame the latest newcomers for ruining our paradise, but it is shortsighted. Truly, what is new is old to the East End of Long Island—and will always be.

—Steven Petrow
Southampton, Long Island
January 2004

Hamptons Timeline

1639   Lion Gardiner makes the East End's first real estate purchase by acquiring the island off East Hampton that still bears his name.

1640s   The towns of Southampton and East Hampton are founded.

1655   East Hampton passes its first restrictive ordinance, forbidding outsiders from working in the village.

1861   An acre of land in Southampton is valued at less than $2 by local American Indians.

1874   Winslow Homer, the son of a Sag Harbor whaler, takes up painting in East Hampton.

1874   The *Sag Harbor Express* warns that the East End "is fast becoming the favorite spot of many."

1875   There are 200 working farms in East Hampton.

1878   Scribner's Magazine sends Tile Club writers and artists to report on East End villages.

1879   Dr. Gaillard Thomas builds one of the first summer cottages in the Lake Agawam district of Southampton. He pays $200 an acre for a 14-acre parcel.

1880s   Regular steamboat service is inaugurated between Manhattan and Sag Harbor, reducing travel time from three days to overnight.

1885   An acre of land in Southampton has "advanced to $1,500."

1886   Southampton's exclusive Meadow Club opens for lawn tennis.

1891   The Maidstone Club, founded by wealthy New Yorkers, makes its debut in East Hampton.

1892   Shinnecock Hills Golf Club opens in Southampton. This parcel of land is now valued at more than $30,000 per acre.

1893   Local historian William S. Pelletreau declares, "The chief business of the Hamptonites is pleasure."

1895   The Long Island Rail Road opens its depot in East Hampton, with through service from Manhattan.

1901   The first automobile motors into Southampton.

1902   Electricity comes to East Hampton.

1907   The last commercial whale hunt concludes off Amagansett Beach.

1910   The East River tunnel opens, allowing Long Island Rail Road passengers to travel to the Hamptons without taking the ferry.

1919   Prohibition is enacted; rumrunners take to the seas off the East End.

1921   Montauk Highway (Route 27) is paved with concrete.

1925   There are 100 working farms in East Hampton.

1926   Rowe's Pharmacy in East Hampton is sold twice in January, doubling in value.

1928   Saks Fifth Avenue opens its Southampton branch.

1931   East Hampton's Guild Hall is opened with much fanfare.

1933   The Maidstone Club serves alcohol for the first time in its history.

1937   Regular air service between East Hampton and LaGuardia begins, reducing travel time to 80 minutes.

1938   The hurricane of September 21 kills hundreds in the Hamptons and destroys 538 trees.

1939   European painters come to East Hampton at the outbreak of World War II.

1949   One of East Hampton's finest homes, the Fens, is demolished, and the estate is carved up into small lots.

1953   Urban planner Robert Moses announces his plan for a "super-expressway."

1972   The Long Island Expressway is complete, but congestion remains a problem.

CHAPTER ONE

THE LOST HAMPTONS

"A Life of Quietness and Peace"

The woods rolled gloriously over the hills, wild as those around the Scotch lakes; noble amphitheaters of tree-tufted mountains, raked by roaring winds, caught the changing light from a cloud-swept heaven; all was pure nature, fresh from creation. The beach they skirted was wild and stern, with magnificent precipices.

—Scribner's Magazine, 1879, describing the East End of Long Island

While every recent generation believes that it has discovered the beauty and charm of the East End, only to see it marred if not scarred by the next influx of newcomers, there is always a "before." Before the Long Island Expressway tore through the farmlands in the 1960s and 1970s, before the post–World War II Abstract Expressionist artists decided to call East Hampton home, before the Long Island Rail Road carried wealthy "summer people" directly from Manhattan to the East End in the 1890s, before the Tile Club Artists first discovered the Hamptons in the 1870s, creating the first real buzz—before all this, the East End, as most referred to the South Fork of Long Island, was the primitive yet picturesque paradise we can still glimpse today.

The celebrated poet Walt Whitman, often a visitor to the South Fork towns in the mid-1800s, could not contain his wonder, and his poetic descriptions ring alive with his passion as much today as they did then. "To a mineralogist," he wrote, "[the beaches] must be a perpetual feast. Even to my unscientific eyes there were innumerable wonders and beauties all along the shore, and the edges of the cliffs. The earths of all colors, and stones of every conceivable shape, hue, and density, with shells, large boulders of a pure white substance, and layers of those smooth round pebbles called 'milk-stones' by the country children."

Certainly, Whitman had company. Charles de Kay, a renowned New York Times critic in the 19th century, took pen to paper to describe the East Hampton he cherished. "The village street . . . is very wide and shaded by elms, chestnuts, catalpas, and ailanthus trees of good size. Here and there an old mill turns its drowsy sails or holds its bare vanes quiet against the sky. . . . The woods abound with rabbits, squirrels, opossums, and raccoons . . . and this increase in small game has encouraged the foxes. Now and then as one passes down the rough bush roads a streak of reddish color across the sandy track ahead tells of the presence of the wily one." Always, near the broad plain of the white sand beaches, the booming of the surf reverberated.

In fact, time had stood still for the picture-perfect villages dotting the East End ever since Lion Gardiner, an English military engineer, bought the island in 1639 that still bears his name. Gardiner's purchase of the 3,500-acre Eden from the Montauk tribe, the original inhabitants of the East End, consisted simply of a gun, some rum, and 10 cloth coats. This sale, long considered the East End's first real estate transaction, was a bargain if not a steal, for the shrewd surveyor and his descendants. It also would be the last time prime lots in the Hamptons would be traded for trinkets.

It has long been said of the British-born Gardiner that he enjoyed "the privilege of exclusivity." Of course, living on an island can do just that—and he brought that element with him to the East End. Within a decade the towns of Southampton and East Hampton were founded (in 1640 and 1648, respectively), with their neighbors Bridgehampton, Wainscott, and Amagansett not long behind. Not surprisingly, these newcomers liked their "quaint and queer" villages, and they promptly set about devising ways to keep others out.

As early as 1655, East Hampton locals, protecting their newfound farms and fisheries, passed the first restrictive ordinance forbidding outsiders from conducting business in the village. Writing in the vernacular of the time, the town fathers declared: "Noe inhabitant . . . shall sell . . . except the person bee as the Towne do life of." Nor did the restrictions end there. Town records also prohibited "forigners" from catching shellfish or hunting, making it impossible for anyone other than the locals (themselves recent transplants) to earn a living in the seaside village. However odd these early laws may sound, they proved an eerie harbinger of things to come, setting a precedent of "us" versus "them" that would be repeated countless times over the coming centuries.

Originally residents of the Connecticut colony, these newcomers brought with them the characteristics of their New England neighbors, clannishness and a hesitancy to change. More than anything, these early settlers wanted to be left alone, a dominant East End trait that has survived for generations. "These good people have communicated but little with the wider world," John Howard Payne, East Hampton's revered poet and playwright, wrote in the mid-1800s. He comically noted "that an aged one among them, after having been inveigled into a mischievous young friend's wagon, for the first time, to the neighboring town—is said to have exclaimed in amazement, 'Who could have thought that Amerikey had been so big.' "

For two centuries, through the snows of winter and the waves of summer, the East End villages, geographically isolated and psychologically distant from both Connecticut and New York, stood quiet and verdant, with whaling, farming, and church-going being their main occupations. That isolation prompted New York historian Nathaniel Prime to write in 1845: "[The East End] was so far removed—so difficult of access, and presented so few inducements to wander through its forests and wade through its sands, that for the space of 200 years it remained terra incognita, to almost the whole world."

By 1885, the *East Hampton Star* had reason to look back on an era that was quickly ending. Lamenting the changes already set in motion and holding fast to the past, the paper reported: "Not the least of the charms of East-Hampton is the suggestion everywhere of the past. The town irresistibly carries one back to the days of the first settlers . . . and of the life of quietness and peace [that] passed here."

Sag Pond, from Bridge, Bridgehampton, L. I.

SAG POND, FROM BRIDGE, BRIDGEHAMPTON, C. 1909. Through much of the 19th century, the East End remained an isolated whaling, fishing, and farming community. Still, the natural beauty proved astounding, although early on it was not always recognized. The beaches were sometimes described as a "sandy waste" or an "empty expanse." One visitor could hardly stand the sight of the "succession of disagreeable sand hills, a considerable part of which are blown hither and thither by the winds." Another described the South Fork as a "wild, desolate country, infested by mosquitoes and snakes." Later, others would be more readily seduced. (Eric Woodward Collection.)

Breakers.   Southampton, L. I., N. Y.

BREAKERS, SOUTHAMPTON, C. 1915. Not yet known to the world for the beauty of its beaches, the delicate nature of the light, or its rustic villages, the East End remained largely out of sight and out of mind. Nevertheless, the dunescapes made an impression on this visitor: "The beach, with its broad reaches of sand and foaming surges, its wrecks, sand-storms, mirages, soft colors, and long line of sand-dunes cut into every variety of fantastic shape by the winds, was especially prolific of wild fancies." How could anyone paint the East End's bucolic allure any better? Probably no one could—but that has not stopped writers from Walt Whitman to F. Scott Fitzgerald from trying. (Eric Woodward Collection.)

South Road. Sugarloaf in Distance. Shinnecock Hills, L. I.

SOUTH ROAD, SUGARLOAF IN DISTANCE, SHINNECOCK HILLS, C. 1910. Until the early 1900s, the South Road, now Route 27A, remained a dirt road, often impassable in the winter and in rainy months. In 1703, the Shinnecock Hills, just to the west of the village of Southampton, were leased back to the Indians by the colonists for 1,000 years and an ear of corn. By the mid-19th century, Southampton farmers became unhappy with this arrangement; they wanted the land for pasturing their livestock. In 1859, a deal was made and the town of Southampton took back the land. In 1861, the town proprietors sold the 3,200-acre parcel to an investor for $6,250 (just $2 an acre), and in 1884, this same parcel of land sold again for $101,000 (about $30 an acre). Talk about speculation. (Eric Woodward Collection.)

A GLIMPSE OF SHINNECOCK BAY, SHINNECOCK HILLS, SOUTHAMPTON, C. 1905. Early in the 19th century, travelers spent three days in stagecoaches on the dusty roads between New York City and the East End villages, paying a princely $4 for the uncomfortable journey. Many celebrities of that era endured the 100-mile ride, including U.S. presidents John Tyler and Martin Van Buren, and Daniel Webster and *Uncle Tom's Cabin* author Harriet Beecher Stowe, who sat on piles of straw for a more comfortable ride. (Eric Woodward Collection.)

SOUTHAMPTON, L. I.   Old Sayre House.
The oldest English Frame House in the U. S.
still standing.

OLD SAYRE HOUSE, SOUTHAMPTON, C. 1908. Southampton enjoyed the idea that it was the "oldest English settlement in New York State." It did not really matter to the local residents that Gardiner's Island was settled in 1639 or that Southold, on Long Island's North Fork, was settled in the same year as Southampton, 1640. Southamptonites took pride that the "oldest house in New York State," the homestead of Thomas Sayre built in 1648, stood on its Main Street. Although beloved, by the beginning of the 20th century, the traditional saltbox was collapsing, with no one coming forward to preserve it. In 1913, the house was demolished, and some in Southampton began to realize the fragility of the town's historic character. (Eric Woodward Collection.)

The Old Hayground Windmill
near Southampton, Long Island, N. Y.

THE OLD HAYGROUND WINDMILL NEAR SOUTHAMPTON, C. 1905. In an area virtually devoid of streams and rivers for waterpower, the East End colonists relied on wind to churn their gristmills. First built in 1809, this mill worked steadily at grinding grain until 1919, when it became a tearoom, artist's studio, and gallery. Seen as quaint by the summer people, such windmills soon became ornaments on the lawns of shingle-style cottages. Nine of the windmills still survive on the South Fork—with the Hayground Mill now decorating an East Hampton estate. (Eric Woodward Collection.)

Lumba Lane & Turn-Pike, BRIDGEHAMPTON, L. I.

LUMBER LANE AND TURNPIKE, BRIDGEHAMPTON, C. 1903. With a considerably lower profile than its neighbors, Bridgehampton, founded in 1656 (16 years after Southampton), had its own reputation. Four miles to Sag Harbor, eight miles to Southampton, and six miles to East Hampton, Bridgehampton was certainly the geographic nexus of the East End, but far from the social center. Much later, in the 1870s, Bridgehampton became the transfer stop for passengers traveling to Sag Harbor, East Hampton, and other points east. (Eric Woodward Collection.)

Home Sweet Home and
the Old Wind Mill
East Hampton, L. I.

HOME SWEET HOME, EAST HAMPTON, C. 1910. Built in the early 18th century by the Dayton family, this old house became an icon of the Colonial Revival architectural movement. John Howard Payne, an actor and author who spent some of his childhood in East Hampton, certainly would have known this house, but whether he was actually born or lived in it is unclear. The same can be said of the question of whether this handsome cottage was on his mind when he penned the lyrics for the famous song "Home Sweet Home." Whatever the truth is, the house owes its survival to that historical misconception. In 1927, the village of East Hampton bought the house lock, stock, and barrel, and today it stands as a visual icon of "[t]his quiet, simple, and primitive little community," as Payne described his beloved town two centuries ago. (Eric Woodward Collection.)

Clinton Academy.   East Hampton, Long Island.

CLINTON ACADEMY, EAST HAMPTON, C. 1922. Built in 1784, Clinton Academy became the first accredited high school in New York State. By the late 1880s, when the summer colonists began looking for a meeting place or theater where they could hold their social affairs, they chose Clinton Academy, by then vacant. James Renwick Jr., architect of the Smithsonian Institution, was hired to improve the tired building. The front porch was enclosed, a gambrel roof addition built, and the interior redone. In 1921, summer resident Mrs. Lorenzo E. Woodhouse, East Hampton's so-called "First Lady of the Arts," reached back to the past, demolishing the Renwick additions and restoring the building to its late-18th-century appearance. By the 1920s, Clinton Hall had become the headquarters for the East Hampton Historical Society, which it remains today. (Eric Woodward Collection.)

Schinnecock Light House, Long Island.

SHINNECOCK LIGHTHOUSE, C. 1900. About halfway between the Montauk and the Fire Island lighthouses, the Shinnecock Lighthouse was an important beacon along the south shore of Long Island. Built of brick in 1858, the tower stood tall at 170 feet. Still, many ships came to grief and disaster off these shores. "[F]rom Fire Island to Montauk, a sandbar formed by the undertow runs parallel with the beach about a quarter of a mile offshore," Everett J. Edwards wrote in his story "Whale Off!" explaining that "When the swell is heavy, the heft of the sea breaks on this bar. Vessels stranded on this coast invariably stop on the outer edge of the bar and if of too deep draft, they are apt to get torn to pieces there." From shipwrecks to nor'easters and hurricanes, every generation inhabiting the East End has faced hardship and havoc brought on by man and Mother Nature. (Eric Woodward Collection.)

5864   WRECK ON THE BEACH, EAST HAMPTON, L.I.   ILLUSTRATED POST CARD CO., N. Y.

WRECK ON THE BEACH, EAST HAMPTON, C. 1915. Sag Harbor, a mere eight miles from East Hampton and yet a world apart, enjoyed the economic boom of the whaling industry. For a time in the early 19th century, each year brought greater prosperity. Houses and shops multiplied side by side with warehouses and primitive factories. By 1847, Sag Harbor had realized its largest catch, with more than 30 whalers bringing home a million dollars' worth of sperm oil and whalebone to be used for lamps, candles, and corsets. (Eric Woodward Collection.)

FIELD OF LONG ISLAND CAULIFLOWER, C. 1915. From the 17th century onward, family farming proved to be the backbone of the economy of the East End, known for its loamy soil, open fields, and moderate winters. In 1875, more than 200 family farms operated in East Hampton alone. A half-century later, the number was reduced by half, and by 1960, there were a mere 20 working family farms. A local writer warned as the century came to a close, "Alas, the spirit of the times is creeping over this restful place." (Eric Woodward Collection.)

CHAPTER TWO

THE EAST END

"Fast Becoming the Favorite Spot"

East Hampton is blossoming from a mere country village . . . to a full blown and fashionable dwelling place. . . .
The once quiet resort of the few is fast becoming the favorite spot of many.

—*Sag Harbor Express*, July 1874

As the 19th century unfolded, Gilded Age aristocrats flocked to Newport, Rhode Island, this country's first resort community. By mid-century, the town's formerly pristine waterfront was replete with gargantuan marble palaces and villas, referred to by their owners in a kind of inverse snobbery as "summer cottages." It was not that Newport was any more beautiful than the East End villages; its popularity had everything to do with how easily you could get there.

During the 1870s and 1880s, old-timers in Southampton and East Hampton held fast to the past, even rejoicing in their isolation from New York City. Big city papers like the *Brooklyn Eagle* could not miss pointing to the separate world just 100 miles from New York City. "Easthampton has been particularly isolated from the outside world. This has tended to preserve longer than in any of the other towns local characteristics," the newspaper observed.

A local guidebook, *American Seaside Resorts*, also heaped praise on the locals for clinging to their old-fashioned, if not unfashionable, ways: "[L]et us say that East Hampton is no place for those whose hearts are in this world of fashion, and who cannot enjoy a meal unless it is served in several courses and with due circumstance." Ironically, many of today's Hamptons residents—particularly year-rounders— might feel a twinge of nostalgia for that simpler time.

This insulation from the "ordinary world," as the *Eagle* went on to describe the rest of the United States, was to be short-lived. Change came soon enough in the form of the deluxe steamers that chose Sag Harbor as a destination, opening up the quaint East End villages in the 1880s to "city rovers in quest of sea air and rurality," as East Hampton's native son John Howard Payne wrote. With their elegant staterooms and dining rooms, the liners departed Manhattan late in the afternoon, arriving in Sag Harbor just past breakfast the next morning. Savvy real estate prospectors picked up these well-heeled newcomers, the Hamptons' first "summer people," at the wharf, hustling them in stagecoaches the remaining eight miles to East Hampton.

Those New Yorkers with the means to escape the city spilled out on East Hampton's Main Street with baskets, carpetbags, and leather trunks headed for one of the village's new boardinghouses. A writer from Harper's Magazine, on finally reaching village, described his first reaction to East Hampton, a town so picturesque that it boasted windmills at either end of the main street: "We rejoiced in finding one spot, not far from the metropolis of the New World, that has not felt the improvement of the age; it is just the place to dream away leisure hours."

Scene on the Dock, Sag Harbor. L. I.

SCENE ON THE DOCK, SAG HARBOR, C. 1905. Despite their clannishness, local residents did not have immunity from the wealthy newcomers making their way to the East End by water. Poet John Howard Payne cautioned, "[The summer colonists] stir up extravagant ideas and unsettle the husbandman from his dependence on his plough, by dreams of speculation." Little did anyone know just how stirred up life was about to become. (Eric Woodward Collection.)

THE OLD TOLLGATE BETWEEN SAG HARBOR AND BRIDGEHAMPTON, C. 1905. To take the short trip between villages, passengers paid as little as a quarter or as much as a dollar depending on "the class of service." A tale often told goes like this: "[One day] a salesman asked Jerry Baker [who owned the stagecoach] for a ticket and on hearing the prices said he would take a 25-center. When the stage reached the hill at Snooksville, a much higher hill before it was leveled off, Jerry would stop the coach and call out, 'All those with dollar tickets set still—those with 50 cents tickets get out and walk and those with 25-centers get out—and push.'" (Southampton Historical Museum.)

MAIN STREET AND JOB'S LANE, SOUTHAMPTON, C. 1900. This quiet scene embodies the charming and bucolic qualities that have always been part of the Hampton draw. The elms, the proverbial privet, the unique post fencing, and the understated architecture all combine to create the perfect small-town retreat. At this time the wide lanes were still unpaved, but a watering wagon was never far away if the dust began to fly.

Main Street and Job's Lane, Southampton, L. I.

An 1879 guidebook noted, "The people that go out there in numbers for the summer months have not robbed it of its charms nor modernized it into commonplace." Not yet, at least. (Eric Woodward Collection.)

A Glimpse of the Millpond, Watermill, L. I.

A GLIMPSE OF THE MILLPOND, WATERMILL, C. 1900. "[P]icturesque houses, clean air, surf, bathing in the Atlantic ocean, good society and no mosquitoes, make an ensemble which is East Hampton!" declared the *East Hampton Star* in the 1880s (although the "no mosquitoes" claim was as untrue then as it would be today). Still, the *Star* had it basically right: "What is the charm? I cannot tell you; it is there, that is all I know. Try it for yourself and see." Even the poet Walt Whitman caught the zeitgeist of the East End, sounding more like a real estate promoter than a poet: "It must be confessed that the east end of Long Island for a summer journey affords better sport, greater economy, and a relief from the trammels of fashion, beyond any fashionable resorts or watering places, and is emphatically a good spot to go to." (Southampton Historical Museum.)

Lake Agawam, Southampton, L. I.

LAKE AGAWAM, SOUTHAMPTON, C. 1905. "No one supposed that [New Yorkers] would ever think of building on the 'Necks' west of the town pond," wrote Southampton town historian William S. Pelletreau in 1893 about the pond now called Lake Agawam. At a land auction that same year, 14 acres abutting the lake had come up for sale. One prospective bidder passed on the lot, protesting vehemently, "Too much outside fence, and, besides, it's next to the beach: and the ocean is a bad neighbor." (Southampton Historical Museum.)

Boardwalk to the Beach, Southampton, L. I.

BOARDWALK TO THE BEACH, SOUTHAMPTON, C. 1900. From the earliest days, Southampton's leaders understood the value of publicity in luring more tourists to the East End. An early-1900s pamphlet continued the seduction. "Its beaches are washed by the waves of the broad Atlantic Ocean, whose ever blowing winds temper alike the winter's cold and the summer's heat," sang the town's boosters. Once at the beach, most ladies sat under thatched roof cabanas, holding lace parasols, with their heads covered by wide-brimmed straw hats complete with veils. In an age before lifeguards, the more daring women leaped into the sea, tethered by long hemp ropes to thick poles pounded into the sand. (Eric Woodward Collection.)

BIRD'S-EYE VIEW OF MAIN STREET, SAG HARBOR, C. 1910. For more than 100 years, Sag Harbor, the nexus of maritime trading on Long Island, had eclipsed its more bucolic neighbors to the east and the west, at least in dollars and cents. By 1849, the whale industry was in free fall just two years after its best season ever. Suddenly, petroleum had been discovered in Pennsylvania, as had gold in California, and whale hunters now found the cost of their journeys unprofitable. "Alas. Those stirring scenes of summer are quite over," wrote Prentice Mulford, a Sag Harbor native. "The wharves have gone to decay or sunk in the shifting sands. . . . The ships are for the most part condemned and broken up. . . . All gone." (Eric Woodward Collection.)

ACADEMY OF THE SACRED HEART, SAG HARBOR, L. I.

ACADEMY OF THE SACRED HEART, SAG HARBOR, C. 1910. (Southampton Historical Museum.)

PRESBYTERIAN MANSE, MAIN STREET, SAG HARBOR, C. 1910. Starting in the 1860s, Sag Harbor had both the benefit and alleged curse of gas lighting. Ministers railed against the new "God of Light," fearing that the townspeople would be punished for "defying His laws by turning night into day." The *Sag Harbor Express* understood the deeper meaning of the change, lamenting: "Truly no more can we boast the simplicity and rusticity of the East-Enders. The charm is forever broken, and the Community which has abandoned so far the customs of the 'good old times' as to introduce gas for light, is ripe for anything." (Eric Woodward Collection.)

PRESBYTERIAN MANSE, MAIN STREET, SAG HARBOR LONG ISLAND, N.Y.

THE TOWN POND, EAST HAMPTON, C. 1900. The first white settlers dredged what once had been a low and swampy bog to create Goose Pond (now called Town Pond) at the foot of Main Street. An East Hampton resident described the pond as he saw it back in the late 19th century: "Every morning and evening various herds of milch cows crossed the Green going to pasture on Mill Plain or Lily Pond, returning at nightfall to bathe in Town Pond. . . . [E]very morning after the cows passed the Green, flocks of geese and goslings marched to the Pond. They owned it by day but deserted it when the cattle came back at night." Then, as now, the Town Pond borders some of the oldest homes in the village, surrounded by venerable saltbox houses and windmills, re-creating the spell of a lost village that time has seemingly forgotten. (Eric Woodward Collection.)

MAIN STREET AND POST OFFICE, EAST HAMPTON, C. 1895. Local families took in the first city people as boarders, charging them $8 to $12 a week. At the height of the season, every available room was taken, inciting the *East Hampton Star* to report, "The townspeople exist upon the summer boarder with such whole-hearted zeal that Mr. Lawrence, the miller, has been heard to declare that, 'in summer East Hampton people live by skinning strangers and in winter by skinning each other.' " (Harvey Ginsberg Collection.)

Residence of Stephen Peabody, Southampton, L. I.

RESIDENCE OF STEPHEN PEABODY, SOUTHAMPTON, C. 1900. One of the early boardinghouses, the Peabody House on Southampton's Hill Street, attracted a sophisticated crowd that was drawn to its porches, verandas, and majestic lawn. Ruth Bedford Moran, among the first summer people and daughter of the noted 19th-century artist Thomas Moran, recalled what it was like to be a summer boarder: "The village people didn't want us at first. They were very stand-offish. They would take us into their homes as boarders; but they rented reluctantly and sold only under pressure of necessity." (Eric Woodward Collection.)

Boyhood Home of Henry Ward Beecher,
East Hampton, L. I.

BOYHOOD HOME OF HENRY WARD BEECHER, EAST HAMPTON, C. 1912. For the Reverend Lyman Beecher, one of the 19th century's best-known religious leaders and one of the town's leading citizens, the East End was something of an outpost of civilization. To his eye it consisted of "the plainest farm-houses, standing directly on the street, with the wood-pile by the front door, and the barn close by, also on standing on the street." Of course, it was a scene precisely like that drawn by Beecher that attracted the Tile Club artists of the 1870s (who arguably put the Hamptons on the map) and generations since then. Reverend Beecher's progeny included a son, abolitionist Henry Ward Beecher, and a daughter, Harriet Beecher Stowe, who wrote *Uncle Tom's Cabin*. Even then, the Hamptons attracted the cult of contemporary celebrity. (Eric Woodward Collection.)

5869   WHALE CAPTURED AT AMAGANSETT, L. I. FEB 22ND, 1907. 57 FEET LONG, 15 FEET FROM TIP TO TIP OF FLUKES, SKELETON NOW ON EXHIBITION AT MUSEUM OF NATURAL HISTORY OF NEW YORK N. Y.
PUBLISHED BY WM. M. COOK, SAG HARBOR, L. I.

WHALE CAPTURED AT AMAGANSETT, 1907. The last whale captured by local fishermen came early in 1907, after more than a century of commercial whaling. For many years the bones of this whale, reassembled at the American Museum of Natural History in New York, were mounted on display there, a bittersweet remembrance of things past. (Eric Woodward Collection.)

Moonlight on Lake Agawam, Southampton, L.I.

MOONLIGHT ON LAKE AGAWAM, C. 1910. In the fall of 1893, the *Long Island Magazine* published a seminal article, "The New Southampton," that wistfully noted how quickly the little village had changed. "Farming," it reported, "no longer holds the high position it once held, and in too many cases has been abandoned for what may seem easier methods of making money. . . . That there has been an advance in the wealth of the community is apparent. The change from a struggle for existence to comparative affluence is great." This generation, like so many to follow, bemoaned the loss of the East End as they knew it. (Eric Woodward Collection.)

CHAPTER THREE

AN ENGINE IN THE GARDEN

"All Aboard for the Hamptons!"

Neither natives nor Summer residents want the railroad or a hotel. They like being eight miles from Sag Harbor,
and the same distance from Bridge Hampton. . . . As soon as they have these improvements
they fear East Hampton will become fashionable.

—The *New York World*, August 1890

Both the threat and the promise of the railroad had hung over the Hamptons at least since the 1850s, when a local writer excitedly described the extension of the rail line to East Hampton from Riverhead, about 16 miles to the west. By 1870, the Long Island Rail Road had opened a through line to Bridgehampton, turning the small crossroads of the town into a transfer station for the genteel travelers headed to East Hampton and Sag Harbor.

Not long after, Scribner's Magazine dispatched a band of artists and writers—via train—to depict life on the East End. Known as the Tile Club of New York (every member had to paint a tile upon joining), these bohemians were overwhelmed by the charming villages and seaside vistas, so much so that they made unspoiled East Hampton their summer home. For them and for anyone who read "The Tile Club at Play," the merry account of their journey, the landscape was "a painter's gold mine" full of windmills and 17th-century saltbox cottages. "[The town] is like a vignette perpetuated in electrotype," the article noted. Not long after the artists' invasion, one wealthy resident prophesied, "Like Bar Harbor, East Hampton was discovered, so far as the Summer colony goes, by artists, who are always looking for new, attractive, inexpensive places. I don't say that East Hampton will ever become a second Bar Harbor, but it has begun on the same lines and has the advantage of being very much nearer New York."

Meanwhile, the *East Hampton Star*, the unofficial voice of the village, could not have beaten the drum any more loudly for the railroad extension. In an 1891 story entitled "Leave No Stone Unturned," the paper advised that "[n]o one should spare any efforts to attract the city people to our town. Those who contemplate taking summer boarders during the coming season are asked to furnish in writing to the nearest station agent all details—or incorporation in a pamphlet . . . to be issued by the Long Island Rail Road."

Others feared the impending change: cows might be disturbed; the area's rustic charm could well be ruined. What exactly was that charm that town folk pined to preserve? One observer rather sharply described the area's vein of exclusivity: "[The town is] innate with good breeding and good family; [there is] no vulgar parvenu that so often makes life wretched at the conventional summer resort. . . . Six miles to the railroad keeps off the outside rabble." A letter to the editor published in the *Star* also minced no words: "[We are] desirous of attending to [our] business and allowing others to attend to theirs."

Even James Fenimore Cooper, one of the best-known American writers of the 19th century, got caught up in the fray, warning, "How many delightful hamlets, pleasant villages, and even tranquil country towns, are losing their primitive characters for simplicity and contentment, by the passage of these fiery trains, that drag after them a sort of bastard elegance."

In the end, the railroad conquered the Hamptons forever, muting the issue of whether the remote villages of the East End would remain a separate world. Both full-time residents and the growing number of summer colonists tried to balance their desire to become a resort community with the "quiet, simple and primitive" community they had known for generations. A local chronicler summed up the dilemma at hand: "East Hampton is in the trying position of wanting to have its cake and eat it too."

MONTAUK HIGHWAY ALONG SHINNECOCK BAY, SOUTHAMPTON, C. 1925. Montauk Highway became the major route for farmers on the East End to get their cattle to and from the fields at Quogue and the other western pastures. For those coming by stagecoach in the mid-19th century, this lovely bend between the Shinnecock Hills and the beach would have been the first real vista of water after many miles of travel. As overland travel became more frequent, the locals began to fret, as others would in the future. One of those voices, the *Sag Harbor Express*, grimly concluded, "In Suffolk County there is a new thing under the sun, and progress is now the watchword. . . . [Any attempt to resist] is in vain." (Southampton Historical Museum.)

MAIN STREET, EAST HAMPTON, C. 1900. A group of East Hamptonites concerned about preserving property values and the town's character exactly as they *imagined* it to be wrote to the president of the Long Island Rail Road in September 1882 in an attempt to prevent the iron horse from reaching their town (an early case of NIMBY, or "not in my backyard"). Not surprisingly, they did not object to the train going directly to Bridgehampton or Sag Harbor, but, please, not to their East Hampton. "We respectfully call to your attention the ultimate damage the citizens would sustain, by reason of the deterioration in value of property in the village, and to the fact that the peculiar charm this village possesses as a sea-side resort will be completely destroyed." (Eric Woodward Collection.)

The Railroad Station, East Hampton, L. I.

THE RAILROAD STATION, EAST HAMPTON, C. 1898. In spite of protest from residents, by 1887, local businessmen obtained a station site and convinced the Long Island Rail Road to extend the rail line into East Hampton. And so it was on May 4, 1895, at 3:16 p.m. that the first Long Island Rail Road coaches pulled into the East Hampton depot—only half an hour late. Although faster than steamboat service, the train ride was far less luxurious, especially to Mary Hamlin, a founder of the East Hampton Riding Club: "The poet's rare day in June was a perfect inferno that fateful Saturday we boarded the evil-smelling old 34th Street Ferry to Long Island City, there to buy our epoch-making first ticket to the then completely unknown East Hampton. . . . But what we suffered to get there! Four hours of torture from suffocating clouds of smoke and dust (no oiled roadbed then), prostrating heat from parboiled cars, and endless jerky stops at every crossroad." (Harvey Ginsberg Collection.)

Main Street,
showing Post Office and Bank,
Southampton, L. I.

MAIN STREET, SHOWING POST OFFICE AND BANK, SOUTHAMPTON, C. 1918. The public found itself torn when it came to the question of progress. An 1885 article in *Harper's New Monthly* spotlighted this ambivalence, noting that many who opposed the railroad benefited from the "uninvited sojourners" and their material prosperity. The *Harper's* article continued: "[While] the Southampton village of this year is an altogether charming place, [a] certain forefather of the hamlet is said to hold a different opinion. He sadly shakes his head and says that it 'does not seem like his old home, with all these carriages going up and down the street.' Perhaps not; but he ought to find a certain consolation in the fact that land has advanced to $1500 an acre." (Eric Woodward Collection.)

52 THE VILLAGE FAIR, EAST HAMPTON, L. I.

THE VILLAGE FAIR, EAST HAMPTON, C. 1905. "The grounds presented a very animated scene," reported the *East Hampton Star* in August 1886 on the occasion of a Ladies' Day Tea, the work of the East Hampton Ladies Village Improvement Society to raise funds to beautify the town. Although usually a strong proponent of progress, the *Star* flinched in this instance: "The sight was exceedingly attractive but it nevertheless led to a cool shudder and the question: Is East Hampton becoming a fashionable summer resort? Certainly this is not the rural simplicity which is so soothing to the mind." Even at this early date, the price of progress was beginning to be understood. (Harvey Ginsberg Collection.)

Ball Grounds, East Hampton, L. I.

BALL GROUNDS, EAST HAMPTON, C. 1920. East Hampton celebrated its 250th anniversary in 1899 with a memorial parade and flag raising. Looking predominantly to the past, the parade consisted of "floats and four-horse teams," "double and single rigs," a "bicycle brigade," and scores of equestrians, many in 17th-century costumes. A special float carried children, who raised the Stars and Stripes at the new Liberty Pole at Main Street and Buell's Lane. According to the *Star*, the only children eligible to participate in the flag raising were those who were "direct descendants in the eighth and ninth generations from the first settlers who laid out the town on this spot in the spring of 1649." (Harvey Ginsberg Collection.)

Along the Town Pond, East Hampton, Long Island, N. Y.

ALONG THE TOWN POND, EAST HAMPTON, C. 1912. By the 1890s, real estate promoters had started selling off the farms to make way for residential developments. One property listed as "a large, elegant Queen Anne country seat with barn, carriage house, plus ice house on 10 acres" sold for $24,000, a considerable sum at the time. Other changes were in the offing, too. In June 1901, the first automobile lumbered down East Hampton's Main Street, causing two young women to be thrown from their horse carriage. That summer the papers reported that a local resident "is out on the street nearly every day with his Locomobile. Horse owners hire him up to run up and down the street while they accustom their animals to the machine." Yet again, it was feared that the "quaint, queer, quiet" town, as one visitor referred to East Hampton in 1894, would be no more. (Eric Woodward Collection.)

South Main Street, Southampton, L. I.

SOUTH MAIN STREET, SOUTHAMPTON, C. 1912. In 1902, the town of Southampton faced its first road-building controversy. Directly acknowledging that the summer colony was now the primary source of revenue, the town determined to "cultivate this source of general prosperity." Its report concluded, "No single expenditure of public money . . . begins to compare with judicious expenditure for the first class improvement of roads." Others were not so sure and became increasingly vocal in their opposition. (Eric Woodward Collection.)

Waiting for the Bathers, East Hampton, L. I.

WAITING FOR THE BATHERS, EAST HAMPTON, C. 1920. The *East Hampton Star* never let a week go by without mentioning the deplorable state of the town's roads, swirling with dust in the summer, knee-high with snow in winter. In 1905, East Hampton approved its first special bond issue for $100,000 to pave Newtown Lane, one of the village's main thoroughfares. As with all progress, there were critics. In 1899, the Home Electric Company was established, with the summer people strenuously objecting to the introduction of electric streetlights in the "quaint old East End Town's streets." Locals took exception with the summer colonists in what would be one of many ongoing battles over the course and character of the town. On this issue, at least, a happy compromise was reached: the electric lines went in, but the summer colonists insisted on underground wiring on Main Street to preserve the beauty of the village. (Eric Woodward Collection.)

Bathing Beach   Southampton, Long Island, N. Y.

BATHING BEACH, SOUTHAMPTON, C. 1920. With the dawn of the new century, the so-called tourist trade increasingly took precedence over farming. "[The] change of conditions in the past twenty-five years has made the summer resident population largely the source of income . . . for the whole community," Southampton town officials announced, following quickly on the *Brooklyn Eagle*'s 1899 proclamation "It may now be said with all seriousness that the chief business of the Hamptonites is pleasure." (Eric Woodward Collection.)

M-16   FERRY LANDING, SHELTER ISLAND HEIGHTS, N. Y.

FERRY LANDING, SHELTER ISLAND HEIGHTS, C. 1910. Not exactly one of the Hamptons, Shelter Island lies three miles from Sag Harbor in the midst of the Great South Bay. In 1878, a writer for *Our Neighborhood*, a Long Island broadsheet, discussed his impending visit to Shelter Island with his wife: " 'Shelter Island?' said my wife. 'I've heard of that place. Let me see; where is it? How do you get there? Is it a fashionable place?' " Off they went, via train and ferry. The wife, both "charmed" and "enraptured" by the island, exclaimed to her husband, "[D]id you ever see such a view as that in all your life?" Apparently many agreed, and it did not take long before crowds at the Shelter Island ferries became commonplace on summer weekends, a legacy alive and well today. (Eric Woodward Collection.)

PARKING PLACE FOR AUTOS. R. R. STATION SOUTHAMPTON, L. I.

PARKING PLACE FOR AUTOS, RAILROAD STATION, SOUTHAMPTON, C. THE 1920S. In 1910, Manhattan's Pennsylvania Station and the East River tunnel opened, allowing passengers to avoid the time-consuming and disruptive ferry ride. The Cannonball Express brought more weekenders, as did the newly paved roads. Almost overnight the Hamptons became but a five-hour drive from Manhattan. By the end of the 1920s, *Who's Who Southampton/Easthampton* reported that "Southampton [now had] the distinction of being the smartest resort in America." The fast-growing town also realized another first with overcrowded roads and parking lots. (Eric Woodward Collection.)

Week-End Guests Arriving at East Hampton Depot, Long Island.

WEEKEND GUESTS ARRIVING AT EAST HAMPTON DEPOT, C. 1935. Year-rounders continued to regard the summer people, even those who owned their own homes, as outsiders. Jeannette Edwards Rattray, who for decades penned the "Summer Colony" news in the *Star*, wrote with a clever touch of irony about the difficulty outsiders faced in breaking into society. Describing one prominent local family, she recounted, "The Lesters have been in East Hampton *only* about two hundred years." (Harvey Ginsberg Collection.)

CHAPTER FOUR

A SUMMER RESORT IS BORN

"*If You Aren't* in *the Maidstone, You're* out *of It*"

*East Hampton is destined to be the summer home of America's retired gentlemen, whose lavish expenditure will
in the near future revolutionize and embellish this favorite resort. No place has such natural attractions;
no place such beautiful rivers; no place has such pure, invigorating air; no place better water;
and I am certain there is no place better adapted to men of means.*

—*East Hampton Star*, 1890s

Late in the summer of 1891, more than a decade after the Tile Club writers and artists from New York had popularized the beauty of the East End, a meeting was held by "persons interested in the erection of a clubhouse in East Hampton." This first reference to what would become the Maidstone Club, the epicenter of East Hampton society, was quietly reported in the *Star*.

When completed just a few years later, the fashionable club, built on 18 acres majestically overlooking the Atlantic, flaunted a handsome and costly clubhouse as well as a theater, dance hall, and bowling alley. The *Journalist*, a New York publication, succinctly described the East Hampton scene of that era: "You wear fancy blazers, dress a good deal, play tennis and attend hops." The Maidstone Club's members list has included the "best" families, starting with some of its earliest: Juan Terry Trippe, the founder of Pan American World Airways, William Clay Ford of Model-T fame, and the highly popular matinee idol John Drew, the uncle of actors John and Ethel Barrymore (and distant relation to his namesake actress Drew Barrymore). It did not take long before the summer colonists were heard to be saying: "If you aren't *in* the Maidstone, you're *out* of it."

A writer for the *New York World*, in an article ironically titled "Quaint East Hampton," described the radical shift, from pristine and picturesque to swank and swish:

> One need not fancy it dull here. . . . There is a tennis club to which nearly everyone belongs, and once a week one of the matrons serves tea in a little stable on the grounds, which is tastefully decorated with greens, tennis nets, golden rod and other wild flowers. . . . Everybody meets everybody else on the beach in the morning and there is a town hall where every Saturday night a dance is given, where the men wear evening dress and the belles display last Winter's evening dresses. Then there are private card parties, dances and receptions given at the attractive homes of the city residents.

Governed with an iron hand by Dr. Everett Herrick, the Maidstone was far from fun and games. It served no alcohol, banned golf on Sundays (until 1906, and after that date, members could play only after 12:30 p.m.), disallowed the custom of late afternoon tea, and prohibited swimming until Herrick personally approved each and every bathing suit's appropriateness. Herrick's tyranny extended even to the tennis courts. Players had to abstain from drinking water for 10 minutes after finishing their games.

The opening of the Maidstone and of the Meadow Club, in neighboring Southampton, as well as the Shinnecock Hills Golf Club, the all-male Southampton Club and others, signaled the end of the bohemian Hamptons and the entrenchment of a new ruling class on the East End. A longtime observer noted that "the Maidstone Club was the dominant influence in East Hampton life for over half a century. It determined the entire character of the village, its social graces, even its look."

Certainly by the first decade of the 20th century, the Hamptons could no longer be described merely as quaint seaside hamlets, the playground of artists and writers. The next wave of newcomers brought industrialists and financiers—among them some of the most prestigious families of the time, including numerous Vanderbilts, Fords, Bouviers, Auchinclosses, Hearsts, and Mellons. Raising the bar even higher, Southampton's *Blue Book,* an exclusive social directory made up of America's blue bloods, made its debut in 1918. The Hamptons had arrived . . . and would again and again.

The Maidstone Club, East Hampton, L. I.

THE MAIDSTONE CLUB, EAST HAMPTON, C. 1915. According to the *Star*, the Maidstone Club founders purchased 18 acres overlooking the ocean for a very upmarket price of $14,000, or just under $800 an acre. Seen by the paper as the start of a "high-class boom," the Maidstone became the most exclusive and restrictive of the East End society clubs. Not only was the club the social hub of the town, but also "membership was considered such a dire necessity that applicants who were rejected often moved," noted one historian. (Eric Woodward Collection.)

Maidstone Club, Showing Swimming Pool and Cabanas, East Hampton, Long Island.

MAIDSTONE CLUB, SHOWING SWIMMING POOL AND CABANAS, C. 1925. The Maidstone members, the Hamptons' latest wave of invaders, detested being referred to either as "city folks" or "summer colonists" (for they were both), preferring the more genteel "country families." In fact, it was not long before these families found yet another new society. Declaring themselves to be "Old East Hampton," a moniker that accurately belonged to the descendants of the 17th-century settlers, these newer families claimed a heritage that was not rightfully theirs but would be useful in asserting their prerogative in years to come. (Eric Woodward Collection.)

Southampton Beach Club   Southampton, Long Island, N. Y.

SOUTHAMPTON BEACH CLUB, C. 1920. "There is probably no place frequented by New York Society where wealth is more prevalent than at Southampton—or where it will purchase less," Mrs. John King Van Rensselaer, a local socialite, wrote of the summer community. The Southampton Beach Corporation (as it was formally known), opened its doors in 1918 and, like the other society clubs, restricted membership to *Blue Book* blue bloods. Low to the dunes, the clubhouse appeared almost monastic in construction and could easily be mistaken for an outpost of a religious sect—in this case, one consisting mainly of sun worshipers. (Eric Woodward Collection.)

SOUTHAMPTON BEACH CLUB, C. 1920. Behind the simple Spanish Colonial Revival façade of the Southampton Beach Club, wealthy members stretched, swam, and suppered, while the locals frolicked on nearby Cooper's Beach. Mrs. Van Rensselaer, a prominent member of the summer colony, archly pronounced that "Southampton is old-fashioned and is determined to stay so. . . . [It] is composed, for the most part, of people who have been in Society too long to care whether they are fashionable or not." (Eric Woodward Collection.)

Club House, National Golf Links of America   Southampton, Long Island, N. Y.

CLUB HOUSE, NATIONAL GOLF LINKS, SOUTHAMPTON, C. 1915. Golf was introduced in the United States in 1888 in Yonkers, and the Shinnecock Hills Golf Club was established three years later, with the first professionally designed course and a clubhouse designed by legendary architect Stanford White. The National Golf Links of America, adjacent to Shinnecock Hills, opened in 1910, and members of each club had access to both courses. According to a 1913 issue of *Southampton Magazine*, "Luncheons and teas out at the club proved very popular and the introduction of golf seemed to fill 'a long felt want,' " even though its early members were ignorant of the game and had joined primarily for the prestige of belonging to an exclusive club. (Southampton Historical Museum.)

Second Hole   Southampton Golf Club, Southampton, Long Island, N. Y.

SECOND HOLE, SOUTHAMPTON GOLF CLUB, C. 1930. "The climax in Southampton's growth and the reason for its change from a simple country place to a fashionable resort was the discovery that the Shinnecock Hills was a naturally ideal golf links," explained a longtime and hyperbolic Southampton resident at the height of the Jazz Age. Of course, boosters of the Maidstone and Meadow Clubs had made just that same argument a generation before; it seemed as if the Hamptons were in perpetual transition from a "simple country place" to a "fashionable resort." (Eric Woodward Collection.)

The Meadow Club. Southampton. L. I.

THE MEADOW CLUB, SOUTHAMPTON, C. 1905. The wealthy class in Southampton, like their counterparts in East Hampton, took note of the changes to their rural community and sought to create a refuge. In 1887, the Meadow Club opened its doors and offered an alternative to dull croquet matches by introducing a new game called tennis. Practically overnight, the simple shingled clubhouse became a haven for the well-connected and well-to-do. Soon the club could boast 30 grassy lawn-tennis courts, 2 squash courts, a polo field, and a bowling alley. Coachmen ferried club members—the ladies in white dresses, gloves, and ubiquitous straw hats, and the men in white flannels, blue blazers, and boaters—to and from the village. (Eric Woodward Collection.)

SPECTATORS WATCHING TENNIS TOURNAMENT AT MEADOW CLUB, SOUTHAMPTON, L. I.

SPECTATORS WATCHING TENNIS TOURNAMENT AT MEADOW CLUB, SOUTHAMPTON, C. 1895. Like its sister club the Maidstone, the Meadow Club had a restricted membership. It was not until late in the 20th century that blacks or Jews could join. This exclusivity may have prompted *Who's Who in Southampton* to declare in 1928 that "[The Meadow Club] is one of the most ultra-fashionable clubs in the country . . . [giving] Southampton the distinction of being the smartest resort in America." A generation later, concerns about the "wrong kind" of people invading the Hamptons led to the start-up of the East Hampton Protection Society. Its goal was to rid the town of its "undesirables." In the 1950s, when actor-director and summer resident Robert Montgomery demanded to know who these undesirables were, no one would answer. The Academy Award nominee told a crowd, "You're talking about Jews and fairies, it's as simple as that." Times had changed, and the next day the Protection Society was shuttered. (Eric Woodward Collection.)

The Southampton Club, Southampton. L. I.

THE SOUTHAMPTON CLUB, C. 1912. "Centrally located in the heart of the village of Southampton stands the attractive club house of the Southampton Club. No tower, turret or cupola forces itself upon the vision of the beholder, no Queen Anne frills nor excessive ornamentation seizes upon the attention of the passer-by." So began *Southampton Magazine*'s 1912 feature on the all-male Southampton Club, founded in 1899. The well-known architect Grosvenor Atterbury designed the clubhouse just off Hill Street, fronting elegant First Neck Lane. An imposing Colonial Revival building with a barnlike roof, eyebrow dormers, and Palladian windows, it was pronounced "a masterpiece of architecture" by *Southampton Magazine*. The club was certainly no place for "romping children" or "chatting women," the publication reported. "[T]ennis talk and social chat . . . were too distracting for the busy men who came from their offices in the city." More than a century later, the club remains a bastion of maleness. (Eric Woodward Collection.)

First Neck Lane, opened in 1644   Southampton, Long Island, N. Y.

FIRST NECK LANE, SOUTHAMPTON, C. 1905. In 1885, Southampton's First Neck Lane was one of the first village streets to be planted with the now ubiquitous privet hedge, a tried-and-true means to cut the winds from blowing away the fine layer of topsoil. It was also a way of demarking property lines. The owners of Southampton's new cottages followed the tradition, looking more for privacy than for soil conservation techniques. Growing as high as 15 feet, the hedges soon became as much a political as a horticultural statement. In 1934, *Society's Season at Southampton* described the village scene, reporting that "Southampton homes are apt to be recessive, set far back behind towering hedges of privet." (Eric Woodward Collection.)

GATHERING FOR A FOX HUNT, SOUTHAMPTON, C. 1900. The summer colonists took great pains to re-create a familiar class structure in the Hamptons, indulging in tennis, golf, swimming, art classes, and fox hunting. In the 1880s, several hunt clubs developed in and near Southampton. Their red-coated riders were frequently seen charging out of the village toward the Shinnecock badlands to the west, with brass trumpets blaring behind the fox in the lead—very English; the horsy set had come to stay. Today, the Hampton Classic Horse Show is considered one of the country's premier equestrian hunter and jumper exhibitions. (Eric Woodward Collection.)

VIEWS OF GREENPORT, L.I.

VIEWS OF GREENPORT, LONG ISLAND, C. 1910.
Then, as now, rivalries among towns were not
uncommon, especially the frequent jabs between
residents of the North and South Forks (and, of course,
among the Hamptons villages themselves). In 1890, the
local newspaper the *Journalist* added some fuel to the fire
with its lively article "Lovely Long Island." "It makes all
the difference in the world whether you spend your
summer vacation on the North, or South fork," the
paper reported. "The South side abounds in cottages and
summer boarding houses. The North, with farm houses,
the best fishing, and some of the worst hotels in
America." (Eric Woodward Collection.)

CHAPTER FIVE

LIFESTYLES OF THE RICH AND FAMOUS

"Who Is the Most Hampton of Them All?"

None of the old towns that dot the seaward side of Long Island has quite the same air of quiet and picturesqueness
that East Hampton presents. Southampton is too crowded and fashionable.
West Hampton and Quogue too monotonously flat,
Amagansett too straggling and unkempt,
Bridgehampton commonplace by comparison.

—The *New York Times*, 1898

As the new century unfolded, and especially during the 1920s and 1930s, the villages of Southampton and East Hampton developed subtle but prized differences in their characters, citizenry, and architecture. "In Southampton, the houses were bigger, the lawns were broader, and the privet hedges thicker," commented one architectural critic, who also noted that Southamptonites tended toward a more conspicuous display of their wealth. In 1928, Saks Fifth Avenue chose Southampton in which to open its first branch outside of New York City. On its heels, Elizabeth Arden and Charles of the Ritz opened their doors, the latter maintaining a complete beauty salon of "master hairdressers selected from his establishment in the Ritz-Carlton Hotel, New York . . . for the convenience of the summer colonists of the Hamptons."

In East Hampton the bohemian legacy of the 19th-century artists remained, with what one critic noted was "a rarified simplicity in their architecture and gardens." He added that "[h]aving nothing to hide, they were more likely to leave their lawns open to the road." East Hampton continued to be a mecca for both artists and writers. Summer cocktail parties in the 1920s and 1930s often included Zelda and Scott Fitzgerald, Dorothy Parker, and John Dos Passos, and a new wave of artists, from Hollywood: Mary Pickford, Douglas Fairbanks, and the Barrymores—to do some characteristic Hamptons' name-dropping.

Other differences could be noted. East Hampton was more Protestant; Southampton more Roman Catholic. East Hampton had more of an intellectual patina; Southampton's appeal was in its conservative zeal. For two centuries there was no fast rule about how to spell the name of the town originally known as Maidstone, reflecting the town's quiet identity crisis. With many variations—East Hampton, East-Hampton, and Easthampton—it was not until 1926 that the state of New York issued a decree: "Must Spell East Hampton in Two Words." Southampton had no such troubles and, since 1640, has stuck to the one-word form.

Competition has loomed between Southampton and East Hampton since their agrarian days, with little consideration given to the so-called non-Hamptons: Bridgehampton, Westhampton, and Good Ground (smartly renamed Hampton Bays in the early 1920s). In 1926, the *New Yorker* jumped into the fray, giving Southampton the nod over its rival village to the east. "Even in the remote days—there were three places to go: Newport, Southampton, and Bar Harbor—they have all grown larger," the magazine reported. It continued, "Southampton has given birth to East Hampton." However, Alice Terbell, a longtime East Hampton resident, would have none of the *New Yorker*'s heresy: "Given birth indeed!

The summer people came here first [to East Hampton]. They were coming eighty years ago when I was a small child, and Southampton was a lonesome enough place. . . . The road from Sag Harbor to here was better and not so long as to Southampton, so they still came here. . . . East Hampton was always lively, and dignified too, for the very best people came here."

The Dunes, Looking West, Southampton, L. I.

THE DUNES, LOOKING WEST, EAST HAMPTON, C. 1910. The Reverend T. DeWitt Talmage, one of many prominent ministers to come to the East End, fell in love with East Hampton. Every week, his sermons were published to a growing readership in the *New York World*, creating even more of a buzz about the pristine beaches and quaint town. "Our summer house is a cottage overlooking the sea," Talmage wrote in 1886. "With an Atlantic Ocean in which to wash and a great-hearted, practical, sympathetic Gospel to take care of all the future, who could not be happy in East Hampton?" Such was the Good Word according to the Reverend Talmage. (Eric Woodward Collection.)

Determined to make peace on the East End, *Who's Who Southampton and East Hampton* proclaimed, with a diplomat's or socialite's sensitivity, "It has been said that of all the Hamptons, Southampton is the smartest, East Hampton the quaintest, and Westhampton the most human." This debate continues to rage in newspaper columns, at cocktail parties, and in the packed cars of the Long Island Rail Road.

COTTAGE AVENUE, EAST HAMPTON, C. 1910. Costing about $10,000 (a tidy sum back then) at the beginning of the 20th century, Hamptons cottages were considered simple homes, said to be indicative of the East End's "unpretentious architecture." Compared to Newport's mansions ("so huge and cold-looking that they could be mistaken for an orphanage"), the so-called cottages springing up in Southampton and East Hampton *were* subdued. (Eric Woodward Collection.)

Cottages along the Shore of Georgica Lake, Wainscott, N. Y.

COTTAGES ALONG THE SHORE OF GEORGICA LAKE, WAINSCOTT, C. 1912. As far back as the 1890s, Georgica Lake (as it was called then) attracted its own upscale breed of suitors. Just before 1900, famed American painter Albert Herter and his wife, Adele, took possession of 75 acres of land abutting the pond. They hired society architect Grosvenor Atterbury to build the Creeks, "perhaps the most important house in *all* the Hamptons," according to a social observer. An Italian-style villa topped with a copper roof, it was adjoined by a dozen guesthouses and some of the Hamptons' most extensive and beautiful gardens. The fashionable area, now known as Georgica Pond, is currently home to notables Steven Spielberg, Martha Stewart, and Revlon billionaire Ronald O. Perlman. (Eric Woodward Collection.)

P-1228

SEA SPRAY HOTEL, EASTHAMPTON, L. I.

SEA SPRAY HOTEL, EAST HAMPTON, C. 1905. Early summer visitors to the East End stayed with local families as boarders. In time, many of these homes were not considered grand enough for the summer visitors and, in response, were turned into first-rate hotels. Such is the history of the Sea Spray Inn. Its first incarnation was as an 1840s boardinghouse on East Hampton's Main Street. In the 1860s, an enterprising manager brought the first Sunday newspapers to the Sea Spray (and East Hampton). At the time, delivery of Sunday papers was as big an issue as Sunday golf and Sunday movies would later be: a challenge to the Sabbath. By 1902, the inn's owners decided that the Main Beach would be a more charming location than the town's major thoroughfare, especially since automobiles now motored through the village. The old inn survived many a calamity, finally succumbing to a winter nor'easter in 1978. (Eric Woodward Collection.)

Residence of Ring Lardner, East Hampton, Long Island.

RESIDENCE OF RING LARDNER, EAST HAMPTON, C. 1930. While Southampton cemented its reputation as the "fashionable watering-place for New York's socially elect" in the new century, East Hampton drew a new breed of writers who included Ring Lardner, the noted humorist and screenplay writer, and Grantland Rice, a high-profile sports journalist. Both men were considered among the best and the brightest journalists of their generation. In the 1920s, they built side-by-side oceanfront homes for their families. (Harvey Ginsberg Collection.)

THE OLD AND NEW EPISCOPAL CHURCH, EAST HAMPTON, C. 1909. Although it could hardly be called Gothic fever, East Hampton's summer residents assiduously employed medieval English design around the village green, thinking that it boosted the town's aesthetic appeal. The summer colonists seemed to find inspiration in the erroneous idea that the town's original settlers had come from Maidstone, England. Their ultimate conceit, however, was to construct the new Episcopal church, St. Luke's, in a style that would seem "very Maidstone." Designed by Thomas Nash in 1910, it replaced the 1859 shingled chapel, which was also Gothic but not authentically so. The Nash design was so successful that within a decade the church was being labeled as a "reproduction of [a] Maidstone parish church." (Eric Woodward Collection.)

THE LIBRARY, SOUTHAMPTON, c. 1900. (Eric Woodward Collection.)

The Library, Southampton, L. I.

West Shore of Lake Agawam, Southampton, L. I.

WEST SHORE OF LAKE AGAWAM, SOUTHAMPTON, c. 1900. With cottages sprouting like weeds around Lake Agawam (more than 200 in a decade), Southampton village came to life. By 1900, Rogers Memorial Library, the Parrish Art Museum, and the Southampton bank were all open for business or pleasure. In 1913, *Southampton Magazine* reported on "the many changes that have taken place in our village during the last half dozen years. . . . *The Sea Side Times* has changed hands. The First National Bank has been organized. . . . The old Sayre house, which was the oldest house in New York state, has been demolished. Two new stores have been built on Job's Lane. Three garages have been built, new cement sidewalks constructed and residences erected all over the village." All that, with more yet to come. (Eric Woodward Collection.)

VIEW OF MAIN STREET, LOOKING SOUTH, SOUTHAMPTON, C. 1925. Mrs. John King Van Rensselaer, author of *The Social Ladder* (1924), commented on what many called "the new Southampton," which was really the old Southampton with a fresh coat of paint. "Its houses have modern conveniences they did not possess a half century ago. Automobiles have taken the place of horses. Apart from these changes, the summer colony stands much as it stood a decade after its foundation, a dignified, aristocratic community of wealthy men and women who live graciously in their pleasant homes, hold aloof from the noise and display of 'modern society,' and turn austere and uncompromising backs on the 'jazz crowd' that now and again makes an unsuccessful attempt to gain a foothold in this last citadel of the old social order." No wonder East Hampton was known to be lively and gay—and Southampton was, well, not. (Eric Woodward Collection.)

The Bathing Pavilion, Southampton, L. I.

THE BATHING PAVILION, SOUTHAMPTON, C. 1910. At the Newport summer colony, the bathing scene, like all social life, was highly orchestrated. "One must wear a certain regulation bathing costume [there]," noted the 1928 *Who's Who*. In Southampton, unlike East Hampton, no such restrictions existed. "The younger set doffs bathing suits . . . some of which are very short indeed. There was a time when the dowagers were a bit shocked by such beach freedom, but they have ceased to raise their eyebrows, and many are downright in favor of it." (Southampton Historical Museum.)

St. Andrew's Dune Church, Southampton, L. I.

ST. ANDREW'S DUNE CHURCH, SOUTHAMPTON, C. 1920. Through much of the 1870s, the Southampton summer colony had only two churches to choose from, Presbyterian and Methodist. In 1879, a prominent summer resident gave an old lifesaving station, plus an oceanfront lot, to be used as a summer church for the cottagers living near Lake Agawam. The church, first named St. Andrew's-by-the-Sea, has been commonly called the Dune Church since 1884. The interior is filled with intricate stained-glass windows, including masterpieces by Louis Comfort Tiffany and John LaFarge. The great hurricane of 1938 did enormous damage to the structure. Even the wooden reed pump organ was blown out a side wall and deposited on the road. Now moved back from the ever-eroding beach, the Dune Church is a cherished survivor of storms of every kind. (Eric Woodward Collection.)

THE IRVING HOTEL,
SOUTHAMPTON, C. 1935.
(Eric Woodward Collection.)

THE IRVING HOTEL'S GARDEN,
SOUTHAMPTON, C. 1940. The Irving
House stood as Southampton's polestar
when it came to attracting the "summer
colony." The Irving, formerly a 12-room
boardinghouse, started its 85-year run as a
hotel in 1889. In its heyday, "Roosevelts,
Vanderbilts, Wannamakers, DuPonts, Fords
and later Bouviers and Kennedys were
listed on the register," noted one of the
hotel's obituaries in the 1970s. "Not
everyone could get a room there, even with
money," the paper commented. Eventually,
the historic hotel grew to some 60 rooms;
but by the 1950s, "the Hotel had become a
haven for the rocking chair set," reported
Dan's Paper, a local weekly. In 1974, the
hotel was razed, a victim of changing tastes
and times. (Eric Woodward Collection.)

ON THE BEACH UNDER THE SHADES, WESTHAMPTON BEACH, C. 1920. According to one of the South Fork's more recent social geographers, the Hamptons "do not include Westhampton . . . and Hampton Bays." To many, the charming towns west of the Shinnecock Canal simply do not rate. Still, *Who's Who at Southampton,* in an apparent act of largesse, did devote a *single line* in its 1928 edition to the "other Hamptons," noting that "Westhampton is the friendliest place of them all; everyone knows everyone else. The crowd is more conservative, yet not so snooty as at Southampton; more sociable, yet not as gay as at Easthampton." (Eric Woodward Collection.)

Canoe Place Inn, on Sunrise Trail, near Southampton, Long Island, N. Y.

CANOE PLACE INN, NEAR SOUTHAMPTON, C. 1925. (Eric Woodward Collection.)

CANOE PLACE INN INTERIOR, C. 1925.
Although the summer residents generally had little appetite for anything west of the canal, the stylish Canoe Place Inn was the exception. The inn's owners, in keeping with the East End's characteristic hyperbole, promoted it as the "oldest hostelry on Long Island." With activities like crabbing, snapper fishing, and snipe-shooting parties, the inn drew people "from the four points of the compass." That was by day. By night, the Jazz Age was in full swing. Society's Season at Southampton gave Canoe Place Inn a big thumbs-up in its 1934 edition: "Night life in the Hamptons will revolve about several brilliant centers. Canoe Place Inn, with its long-established reputation for good food and good music; with Eddie Davis and his Orchestra [will be one of them]." (Eric Woodward Collection.)

GLORIOUS MANSIONS

"Cottages in the Potato Fields"

The only fear that seems to haunt the summer folk in the old camping ground of the Montauks is a speculation whether the time may come for the advent of those who build great places and try to out-do their neighbors in luxury, thus gradually destroying the informal, easy-going life by the sea which still puts East Hampton apart from many other less fortunate watering places.

—Charles de Kay, "Summer Homes at East Hampton, L.I."
Architectural Record, January 1903

Compared with the marble palaces that defined the Newport summer scene, the cottages springing up in Southampton and East Hampton were positively subdued. Charles de Kay, a noted architectural critic, described this new phenomena: "A prevailing type of summer home is a smallish frame dwelling shingled, without paint or stain, having a deep porch cut out from the ground floor. . . . Often there is no stable or barn." However, these houses were no beach shanties; they were the classic shingle-style mansions, many of which still sit atop the Atlantic dunes.

Although considered simple and unpretentious by Newport standards, these new summer residences dwarfed the cozy saltboxes of centuries gone by yet fit in with the lines and curves of the surrounding homes and hills. According to Charles de Kay, "Some of these new houses appear to grow naturally out of the seaside copses and sand grass, and their low-pitched roofs seem to repeat the effect of the sandhills and dwarfed cedars as they crouch and make themselves small before the blast from the ocean."

By any measure they were considered extravagant. The new shingle-style homes had front porches and side porches, ornate parlors and ocean vistas, and an embarrassment of bedrooms, maids' rooms, and sitting rooms. Still, the summer colonists, displaying an uncharacteristic populist sentiment, insisted on referring to them as cottages. In the early days of American resorts, "cottages" described the modest bungalows built around the fancy hotels for overflow guests. Because of their larger size and extra privacy, they became more desirable than the adjoining hotel rooms. In the Hamptons the wealthy and powerful families of influence mimicked the vocabulary of posh resorts like Newport, and so, too, their Hamptons houses became known as cottages.

The new shingle-style homes were generally applauded. Architect Aymar Embury II, who designed the town's library and Guild Hall, commented, "The simple character of these early buildings was never very greatly changed, the new houses followed in a vague sort of way the current architecture of their times without departing very greatly from the simplicity of the older ones." In 1885, a New Yorker bought one of the old houses on East Hampton's Main Street, pushing it back from the street and remodeling it. A writer for the *East Hampton Star* was astonished that the owner decided to keep the original character of the house: "[T]he old time style of finish has been retained, and anyone would think, from a cursory glance at the inside, that he was gazing upon a house in construction many years ago." Embury later concluded that "we had less bad architecture at East Hampton . . . because the . . . tradition of simplicity was strong enough to keep people from the jig-saw atrocities then so common."

By the early 20th century, times were changing, with a new and more ostentatious architectural style taking hold. *Southampton Magazine* reported in 1912 that "[t]he cute little Queen Anne cottage that was so popular in the early days . . . became obsolete . . . and was followed by handsome mansions of colonial or baronial design, set amidst spacious grounds." While the magazine praised these new creations, some were not sure what to think of country seats like Southampton's Villa Mille Fiori, which mimicked the style of the Italian Renaissance, with walls "hung in Venetian red" and floors "finished with satinwood and ebony in a floral design."

At the height of this wave, the *Star* cried, "Some East-Hamptonites have torn down their old homes and built inartistic white monstrosities in their place—convenient, but ugly." Meanwhile, de Kay worried aloud: "How long will Montauk preserve its savage loneliness and grandeur? East Hampton its noble village street? The north woods their shady, sandy solitudes? Sag Harbor its air of an old whaling port?"

(GREY GARDENS) RESIDENCE OF MRS. F.S. PHILLIPS, EAST HAMPTON, C. 1915. "The simplicity and sobriety of the [East End] scenery appears to have influenced the architecture," wrote Charles de Kay in *Architectural Record* in 1903. No better example is Grey Gardens, the residence of Mrs. Stanhope Phillips, designed by Joseph Greenleaf Thorp. Built in 1897 on West End Road overlooking the Atlantic, the house was for years famous for its enclosed back gardens, a monochromatic palette of rare and soft-toned blues, silvers, and grays. Grey Gardens, built for the daughter of the Detroit Free Press's first editor (who belonged to the new monied crowd attracted to the East End), is considered a prime example of de Kay's so-called "simplicity and sobriety." Others have called Thorp's work "banal" and "boring." In the 1920s, the house was bought by the Bouvier family and enjoyed its ultimate celebrity with the national release of the 1970s documentary *Grey Gardens*, featuring Jacqueline Kennedy Onassis's eccentric relations "Big Edie" and "Little Edie." Today, former *Washington Post* editor Ben Bradlee and his wife, writer Sally Quinn, have painstakingly restored the house and gardens. (Eric Woodward Collection.)

Woodhouse Garden, East Hampton, c. 1910. Shown is part of the Japanese garden at the L.E. Woodhouse estate. (Eric Woodward Collection.)

Woodhouse Garden, East Hampton, L. I.

L. E. Woodhouse Cottage, on Huntting Lane East Hampton,

L.E. Woodhouse Cottage on Huntting Lane, East Hampton, c. 1910. Known as East Hampton's first lady because of her passion for the arts, Mary E. Woodhouse, along with her husband, banker Lorenzo E. Woodhouse, was an early member of the Maidstone Club. Together, in 1899, they built one of the most notable homes in town, a village estate known as the Fens. The massive house, more than 12,000 square feet originally, dwarfed its neighbors. "Though a cottage in name," wrote architect Robert A.M. Stern, "[this house] was to be the centerpiece of an elaborate estate, reflecting the shift in family power to the younger generation." In the late 1940s, developers razed the house, and the property was carved up into lots and sold off. (Eric Woodward Collection.)

Residence of Henry A. James, East Hampton, L. I.

RESIDENCE OF HENRY A. JAMES, EAST HAMPTON, C. 1910. As the century waned, the "cottage colony" waxed. Everywhere in East Hampton, it seemed, huge summer cottages were under construction. "The majority of these houses had the so-called Dutch or gambrel roof, probably the shape was vaguely reminiscent of the dune," wrote East Hampton architect Aymar Embury II. Certainly, the Henry A. James cottage (which did not belong to the famous novelist but to a New York lawyer) had gambrels galore. Eccentric and sprawling, the cottage—literally built on the sand dunes—also reflected changing attitudes about East End beaches. Unproductive as far as farming goes, the dunes were perceived to have little value in the 1860s and 1870s. At best, one writer commented, "The dead fish could be spread on the garden for fertilizer." Times were changing. (Eric Woodward Collection.)

Residence of the Hon. Elihu Root, Southampton, L. I.

RESIDENCE OF THE HONORABLE ELIHU ROOT, SOUTHAMPTON, C. 1905. Elihu Root, a New York City lawyer, served in two presidential cabinets and won a Nobel Prize. Built in 1896, this extravagant home boasted numerous dormers and verandas for every vista, and windows of every kind (square, oval, and rectangle, a radical departure at that time). This residence was part of an 1880s "development" surrounding Lake Agawam, which lies between the village and the ocean beaches. Not surprisingly, these shores became one of the most desirable locations for the first summer colonists. Within a short time, "Southampton had become thoroughly established as a perennial place of summer sojourn and the permanency of its efficacy and repute as a health resort had become reliably guaranteed," wrote Charles Jagger in a 1912 issue of *Southampton Magazine*. He added that "there was [also] a marked change in the character of houses erected here. People no longer built 'cottages' . . . but, instead, built 'summer residences.'" (Eric Woodward Collection.)

Residence of H. F. Cook, North Haven, Sag Harbor, L. I.

RESIDENCE OF H.F. COOK, NORTH HAVEN, SAG HARBOR, C. 1900. Once the sole domain of captains and sailors, Hog's Neck, or North Haven, between Sag Harbor and the Shelter Island ferry landing, became a popular site for summering at the end of the 19th century. The rambling Queen Anne style seemed to represent the informal lifestyle of the rich and influential and was the most popular design up and down the eastern seaboard. Many summer residents "could have had more costly homes, had they wished." H.F. Cook, himself not a summer colonist but the owner of the Fahy Watch Case Company in Sag Harbor, no doubt took pleasure in his sprawling mansion, one of a handful of imposing Queen Annes in the area. (Eric Woodward Collection.)

"The Orchard"   Residence of Mr. Charles E. Merrill   Southampton, Long Island, N. Y.

THE ORCHARD, RESIDENCE OF MR. CHARLES E. MERRILL, SOUTHAMPTON, C. 1935. The preeminent architectural team of the time, McKim, Mead & White designed one of the grandest estates in Southampton, the Orchard, for financier James L. Breese. In 1895, Breese hired his friend and architect Stanford White to create a gentleman's estate on his Hill Street property, originally a 30-acre potato farm. The sprawling residence contained 18-foot gilded columns and hand-carved ceilings, and its music room was "decorated in a robber-baron-style of cluttered elegance," according to one local source. The grandiose residence paid homage to George Washington's home in Mount Vernon and certainly evoked an old village saying that claimed "Southampton is for presidents, while East Hampton is for vice presidents." After Breese's wife died, the financier lost interest in the big house and sold it to Charles Merrill of Merrill Lynch in 1935. After World War II, the Orchard again went on the block, this time to find another life as condominiums. (Eric Woodward Collection.)

Residence of J. C. Thaw.   Southampton, L. I.

PUBL. BY CORWITH'S PHARMACY   Hand-colored

RESIDENCE OF J.C. THAW, SOUTHAMPTON, C. 1920. The New York City Thaws built their massive residence, Windbreak, in 1911 on Gin Lane, considered among the most desirable Southampton addresses. The road, dating back to the 17th century, was neither named for the Prohibition-era rumrunners, who did frequent the white sand beach nearby, nor for the summer colonists' drink of choice. Gin Lane was simply the path to the holding gin, a fence-enclosed pasture in which stray cattle were impounded until claimed by their owners. Of course, the path had changed by the time Josiah Copley Thaw built his imposing house by the sea. Thaw's infamous brother, Harry K. Thaw, made national headlines in 1906, when he gunned down architect Stanford White. (Eric Woodward Collection.)

Residence of Mr. H. H. Rogers.   Southampton, L. I., N. Y.

RESIDENCE OF MR. H.H. ROGERS, SOUTHAMPTON, C. 1920. The son of Standard Oil magnate Henry Huddleston Rogers, Henry H. Rogers Jr. certainly did not lack for family money, and his residence Black Point evidences it. Built between 1914 and 1916, this Mediterranean villa, quite unlike its shingled neighbors, sat atop the Atlantic shore dunes, facing the waves. The entire estate was surrounded by a high stucco wall, which both protected the gardens from the wind and sheltered the estate from the only public road on its western side. It was one of a new breed of houses called "stuffy" and "pompous" by some, and its construction led one contemporary observer to observe that "it look[ed] more as if it belonged in Newport. . . ." *Architectural Record* described Black Point's interiors as "splendidly dramatic," housing Renaissance frescoes, rare 18th-century tiles, and exotic wrought-iron work. Still, one Southampton house was not enough for Rogers. He soon built the Port of Missing Men just a few miles away in North Sea as a getaway from summer society. (Southampton Historical Museum.)

Residence of A. B. Boardman.
Southampton, Long Island, N. Y.

RESIDENCE OF A.B. BOARDMAN, SOUTHAMPTON, C. 1920. "[T]here has been a complete and permanent change in the construction of summer residences," reported *Southampton Magazine* in 1912. The subject of the article was Villa Mille Fiori, a high-style Palladian Renaissance house that in its time became known as Southampton's most opulent cottage. In 1910, Albert Barnes Boardman, a Manhattan lawyer, created for his family this version of Villa de Medici, one of Rome's most splendid palaces. Completely constructed out of concrete, the red-tiled mansion boasted an "elaborate living room" and was considered a "conspicuous landmark for many miles in all directions." The magazine also noted: "It is a monolith, fireproof, vermin-proof, [and] heatproof." Alas, the house was not "developer-proof": Villa Mille Fiori was torn down in the 1960s. (Southampton Historical Museum.)

Sunken Garden, "Bayberry Land" Summer Home of Mr. and Mrs. Dwight F. Davis, Sr.
Southampton, Long Island, N. Y.

SUNKEN GARDEN, BAYBERRY LAND, SOUTHAMPTON, C. 1925. Of the highly cultivated estates in the Hamptons, Bayberry Land is among the most famous. Built on a Shinnecock Hill bluff overlooking Peconic Bay, this English Arts and Crafts–style stucco cottage with Georgian interiors was a natural extension of an English country manor house. No detail at Bayberry Land was overlooked. An observer described the mansion's crown: "The roof, of thick rusticated Welsh slate was designed with a bowed slouch in it to suggest that sought-after look of an ancient Devon manor house." Bayberry Land clearly personified a new trend among newcomers to the East End. "As the summer crowd got fancier, it seemed to get more Anglophiliac," a writer for *American Architect* commented. (Eric Woodward Collection.)

The Castle in Pinewold Park, Westhampt n, L I.

THE CASTLE IN PINEWOLD PARK, WESTHAMPTON, C. 1910. The creation of master potter and sculptor Theophilus A. Brouwer Jr., this castle in Pinewold Park is unique in the Hamptons. Since its foundation was laid, the Castle has turned heads and often been called a building "out of place in period and style." Critics notwithstanding, Brouwer, who first arrived in East Hampton in 1894, made extraordinary pottery that was hand-thrown and glazed with magnificent colors and textures. His work quickly caught the attention of Tiffany's, and it has long been rumored that Macy's offered him a million dollars for an exclusive line, which Brouwer allegedly declined. In 1903, the journeyman-turned-potter moved to Westhampton and started building his castle. Brouwer died in 1932, but his house lives on, as does his pottery. (Southampton Historical Museum.)

The Old Windmill House, Southampton, L. I.

THE OLD WINDMILL HOUSE, SOUTHAMPTON, C. 1905. Even before Martha Stewart's infamous tag sales, the quest for curious and quaint objets d'art has long driven the East End's antiquarians and collectors. Early in the 20th century, summer residents could be found knocking on the doors of the old Main Street houses, hoping that the owners might part with a tired musket or a setting of flow-blue china, a rare type of English earthenware. More aggressive summer colonists hunted for larger historic trophies, such as antiquated cottages, barns, or even windmills. One such early summer colonist, Willis Betts, purchased the old Good Ground Windmill in 1880 and moved it from Hampton Bays (which Good Ground was named in the 1920s) to his oceanfront estate on Southampton's Meadow Lane, where it became a guest cottage. Some saw this adaptive reuse as clever; others saw such tinkering with local artifacts as insensitive. For visiting artists and tourists, the Old Windmill House soon became a favorite place in Southampton to paint a picture or snap a photograph. It still is. (Eric Woodward Collection.)

Rowe's Pharmacy   East Hampton, Long Island, N. Y.

ROWE'S PHARMACY, EAST HAMPTON, C. 1930. The mid-1920s saw an unprecedented boom in real estate prices. Each week, the *East Hampton Star* reported on some new deal. "Charles F. Murphy Estate, Sold for $95,000, Resold for Million Dollars," hollered the paper early in 1926. New streets were paved; new subdivisions created; contractors worked day and night. One local article noted the flurry of activity: "There is considerable building going on, making work and wages for our mechanics, who thus are benefited as well as the merchants who are busy supplying the wants of the summer residents." The talk of the town, however, was the site where Rowe's Pharmacy came to be: the corner of Main Street and Newtown Lane. This property sold on January 15, 1926, for over $60,000. By month's end it sold again for an astounding $120,000. Some believe that with this one incident of outrageous speculation, the public perception of the value of East End real estate changed forever. (Harvey Ginsberg Collection.)

RESIDENCE OF WARREN WHIPPLE, HUNTTING LANE
EAST HAMPTON, LONG ISLAND, N.Y.

RESIDENCE OF WARREN WHIPPLE, EAST HAMPTON, C. THE 1930S. Once part of Greycroft, the Lorenzo G. Woodhouse residence, this house was originally the windmill for the vast estate's water supply. Built in 1894, the wind pump was knocked down twice in winter storms during in its first year of construction. By the middle of the 20th century, the combined factors of the Great Depression, the severe hurricane in 1938, and gas rationing during World War II had caused a number of the area's large houses to be razed. Such was the fate of Greycroft. The estate was broken up into several lots, and Windpump Tower (owned by Enez Whipple, longtime director of Guild Hall) found a new home on Huntting Lane. During Windpump Tower's extensive remodeling, a local worker was heard to exclaim, "My God, some people will live in anything!" (Eric Woodward Collection.)

View of Lily Pond Lane, East Hampton, L. I.

VIEW OF LILY POND LANE, EAST HAMPTON, C. 1918. Even after the onset of the Great Depression, fashionable homes held their value. One Lily Pond property sitting on 45 lush acres with a 20-room frame house and a five-car garage, came on the market in the early 1930s for $33,000. The sale pamphlet read, "There are 17 acres of lawns, with graduating terraces reaching down to a spring lake . . . that [suggests] the name 'Lily Pond.' [It] is well-sheltered in an interesting setting of grand old heavily foliaged trees. This ideal location must be seen to be appreciated." During the height of the 1920s real estate boom, the *East Hampton Star* issued a stern warning: "[W]e can only hope that prosperity will not destroy East Hampton as it finds its way to a favored few. . . . East Hampton could very easily be made into a combed and manicured suburb—a New Rochelle—but it must not happen!" (Eric Woodward Collection.)

CHAPTER SEVEN

BEYOND RICH AND FAMOUS

"The Cradle of American Art"

In East Hampton, the artists could be identified from afar, by their suits of velveteen in a soft dark brown with knee-breeches;
hand-knit ribbed heavy stockings, and beret completed the costume. Art became the fashion for the entire summer colony.
Farmers of East Hampton could hardly get out of their own barnyards to milk the cows in the 1880s.

—*Fifty Years of the Maidstone Club, 1891–1941*

By the end of the 1870s, the first wave of artists, a group of painters from New York's Tile Club (with a writer from *Scribner's Magazine* in tow), had descended on the South Fork. They came for the beauty; they recorded the beauty; they created beauty in their work. In turn, these artists forever changed how people valued and perceived the East End's dunes and beaches. Only a few years before, visitors had described the area as a "succession of disagreeable sand hills" and a "wild, desolate country, infested by mosquitoes and snakes." In the artists' eyes (and through their paintings and essays), they caught the essence, if not the soul, of the Hamptons and "its whirling mills, its silvery, silent beaches, its watery marshes and bays."

The early bohemians who took up residence, mainly in East Hampton, were among the nation's best-known and most admired painters, illustrators, and etchers. Winslow Homer, a direct descendant of a Sag Harbor whaler, arrived before the others in 1874, finding inspiration and needed peace and quiet. Renowned painter Thomas Moran, best known for his dramatic panoramas of Yellowstone National Park, fell in love with the village of East Hampton and was soon joined there by Childe Hassam and Albert Herter, equally famous in their time.

By 1883, *Lippincott's Magazine* referred to the seaside village as an American Barbizon, comparing it to the French hamlet outside of Paris known for its naturalistic landscape painters and paintings. Everywhere, it seemed, painters with their makeshift easels could be found recording the area's "antique rural charm," as Thomas Moran described the fields and farmlands. In 1891, painter William Merritt Chase, another Tile Club member, founded the nation's first outdoor art school, known as the Shinnecock Summer School of Art, just outside the village of Southampton. Already a well-established figure in the New York art world, Chase brought his philosophy to the East End, exhorting his students to "play with your paint, be happy over it, sing at your work."

The East End art scene, which started with the Tile Club invasion, spawned a second act early in the 20th century. With a summer colony of great means, local citizens became concerned that there was not sufficient local culture. After traveling in Italy during the summer of 1896, lawyer Samuel L. Parrish had "the thought of establishing this small museum here in the Village of Southampton." Opened in 1897, the museum quickly became, along with Rogers Memorial Library, among the village's most important cultural landmarks.

After a lull during World War I, the much-ballyhooed 1931 opening of East Hampton's Guild Hall, plastered atop the *New York Times* "Society News," marked the beginning of a new cultural era for that village. World War II brought yet another artistic chapter to the East

End, notably the arrival Abstract Expressionist painters such as Jackson Pollock, Robert Motherwell, and Willem de Kooning. "Pop went the Hamptons!" declared one art critic.

By the early 20th century, the marriage of art and celebrity was a fait accompli. The Hamptons were established as not only a home for the rich and famous but also a place where wealthy socialites and struggling artists freely inhabited the same smart salons and parties.

The Old Mill, East Hampton, L. I.

THE OLD MILL, EAST HAMPTON, C. 1900. For the Tile Club members, the South Fork, especially East Hampton, was "a painter's gold mine." The other Hamptons, the members implied, were already spoiled but not this one: "[East Hampton] is like a vignette perpetuated in electrotype." Ruth Bedford Moran, daughter of painter Thomas Moran, suggested how important the artists were to the future development of the village: "[The artists] took away with them on canvas, copper or paper, the essence that was old East Hampton to scatter it over the cities and towns . . . everywhere." (Eric Woodward Collection.)

Summer Residence of Thomas Moran, East Hampton, L. I.

SUMMER RESIDENCE OF THOMAS MORAN, EAST HAMPTON, C. 1910. By the 1880s, the artists' assault on East Hampton was complete. The *Century Magazine* referred to the hamlet as "a true artist colony," with renowned landscape painter Thomas Moran and his wife, Mary Nimmo, also a noted artist, the de facto leaders. In 1884, the Morans constructed the first combined studio-residence just across from what is now known as Town Pond. With a family of 16 talented painters and printmakers, the sizable Moran clan, by itself, made up East Hampton's first art colony. (Eric Woodward Collection.)

THE FREE LIBRARY, EAST HAMPTON, c. 1915. (Eric Woodward Collection.)

INTERIOR OF EAST HAMPTON LIBRARY, C. 1915.
East Hampton's first library was founded at Clinton Hall in 1897, but early in the 20th century, Mary E. Woodhouse, the town's earliest and most steadfast arts supporter, bought the land of the present site on Main Street and commissioned summer resident and architect Aymar Embury II to submit plans suggesting different styles for the new library. One plan called for a Jeffersonian-Palladian structure with a charming cupola; another was more of a stripped-down Beaux-Arts edifice with lovely big windows; the third (and winning) plan was a pure example of rural Elizabethan design. Half-timbered with bay windows, huge gable-end chimneys, and a massive roof that feigns thatch, the new library advanced the summer colonists' quest to establish a little piece of merry olde England right on Main Street. (Eric Woodward Collection.)

INTERIOR OF LIBRARY, EAST HAMPTON, L. I.

Residence of Grantland Rice, East Hampton, Long Island

RESIDENCE OF GRANTLAND RICE, EAST HAMPTON, C. 1930. Sports journalist Grantland Rice was among a handful of prominent writers, including humorist Irwin S. Cobb and drama critic Percy Hammond, who summered in East Hampton during the 1920s and 1930s. Rice regularly used his East End experiences in his work. From his porch, perhaps with a pitcher of gin and tonic nearby, he wrote of the view, "[W]e could stare straight out into the bull rings of Lisbon . . . or perhaps it was the clearness of the gin cocktails. At any rate, nothing but gulls, whales, and water separated us from Portugal and Spain." Although the East End had matured much by the 1920s, Rice—and many writers to come—continued to find inspiration from the land and the sea. (Harvey Ginsberg Collection.)

GUILD HALL, EAST HAMPTON, C. 1935. The 1931 opening of East Hampton's Guild Hall brought praise to all involved: the building's architect, Aymar Embury II; Ruth Dean, a landscape designer (and Embury's wife), who designed the magnificent gardens; and Mary E. Woodhouse, the patron saint of the new arts center. The main gallery was dedicated to painter Thomas Moran, who was rightfully applauded for putting East Hampton and its art colony on the map. With elegant galleries and a state-of-the-art theater, Guild Hall opened the door to East Hampton's artists and art scene, providing a glamorous showcase for their work. Its first exhibit was a retrospective of the works of Tile Club artists, the bohemian painters who had "discovered" East Hampton back in the 1870s. (Eric Woodward Collection.)

John Drew Residence, East Hampton, Long Island, N. Y.

22647

JOHN DREW RESIDENCE, EAST HAMPTON, C. 1915. Actor John Drew, known as "the Aristocrat of the Theater" for his dashing style on and offstage, summered in East Hampton for 30 years. He frequently officiated at local fashion shows and Fourth of July parades. Uncle to Lionel, John, and Ethel Barrymore, Drew built his cottage, which had 4 porches and 12 bedrooms, on Lily Pond Lane in 1902. Named Kyalami, which means "home" in the Zulu language, the house stood a mere 500 feet from the surf. The Drews, like many other wealthy families, had a portable beach house rolled down to the beach each season. Unlike most others, the Drews' pavilion was an exact replica of their own home. In 1931, the theater in Guild Hall was named after the actor, who had died in 1927. (Eric Woodward Collection.)

The Art Village, Southampton, L. I.

THE ART VILLAGE, SOUTHAMPTON, C. 1905. In 1890, amateur artist and Southampton summer resident Mrs. William Hoyt invited American Impressionist artist William Merritt Chase to visit her home on Long Island. Within two years the Shinnecock School of Art, founded by Chase, had opened its doors. Its curriculum emphasized the avant-garde French Impressionist idea of painting real landscapes, not romanticized ones, outdoors from start to finish. The communal studio was located at the hub of the picturesque Art Village, consisting of a cluster of cottages. In 1892, a writer for *Harper's Monthly Magazine* reported on Chase's experiment: "The simple country people have never found anything to admire in the Shinnecock Hills themselves. . . . To them, the . . . Hills have always been rather unlovely, as they are not fertile, and the sandy roads of even a few years ago made travel very hard across them." (Eric Woodward Collection.)

Residence of S. L. Parrish, Southampton, L. I.

RESIDENCE OF S.L. PARRISH, SOUTHAMPTON, C. 1905. New York lawyer and philanthropist Samuel L. Parrish bought this Greek Revival residence on the corner of Southampton's Main Street and Meeting House Lane in 1899. As soon as Parrish took possession, he began enlarging the house. By 1920, he had doubled its size, with wings to the north, south, and east. In 1952, the Parrish residence became the Southampton Historical Museum. (Eric Woodward Collection.)

Parrish Art Museum.   Southampton, L. I.

**PARRISH ART MUSEUM,
SOUTHAMPTON, C. 1925.**
(Eric Woodward Collection.)

Art Museum Grounds, The lily pond, Southampton, L. I.

**ART MUSEUM GROUNDS, THE
LILY POND, SOUTHAMPTON,
C. 1925.** *Architectural Record* took
note of the new museum in a 1915
issue: "The attendance record for
1914 is startling—no fewer than
six thousand persons, and that
during a season only four months
long. More remarkable is the
circumstance that this represents
an attendance considerably in
excess of one hundred per cent
of the maximum summer
population of Southampton."
(Eric Woodward Collection.)

"Good-Bye, Potato Fields"

Amagansett still lives, somehow, on fish; Bridgehampton, on potatoes, and East Hampton, on history; but in the words
of a Clam-digger [native Southamptonite], "This town is going to hell in a Cadillac." The big iron ball
of the house-wrecker has crashed through the monster pavilions of Bar Harbor and Newport.
Southampton's turrets still stand, but the barbarian is at the gates. "See it now, friends,"
said the quidnunc [local], "before the auctioneer brings his hammer down."

—Park East, the Magazine of New York, August 1952

Despite decades of hand-wringing about the railroad, paved roads, city people, and summer colonists, residents of the Hamptons prior to World War II truly thought that the "life of quietness and peace" described by the *East Hampton Star* in the 1880s would prevail. Until the war, locals bought their papers at Ben Barnes's store or sat at the soda fountain at White's Drug Store in East Hampton. Down the road in Southampton, the ducks came to Lake Agawam and the trains to the depot with a regularity (and a regular tardiness) that proved calming. Each generation adapted to the changes, forgetting the struggles that had come before.

By 1945, however, the rhythms of daily life began to move faster and faster. "Plane Hampton–N.Y. Air Express" takes flight, reported the *Star*, amazed that commuters could reach 42nd Street from Main Street in just 80 minutes. In the early 1950s, Robert Moses's plan for a "super-expressway" traversing the island was announced, igniting a controversy unlike any since the railroad invasion in the late 19th century. "We cannot solve our problem just by widening existing highway routes," asserted one public official. "The ultimate solution will only come by the building of a new, modern expressway or throughway on entirely new locations," he added. By the time the Long Island Expressway was completed in 1972, more than $280 million had been sunk into the six-lane roadway that rolled down the middle of the island for 81 miles. Homes were demolished; land prices soared; as fast as the road was built, it was filled with cars.

The East End's cultural landscape also took on new significance, with the arrival of Abstract Expressionist artists Jackson Pollock, Lee Krasner, Robert Motherwell, and others, who found a vision and a home in the midst of the rapidly vanishing potato fields. Once again artists were reinventing the East End scene and, through their art (and escapades), publicizing the Hamptons to the rest of the United States and the world. Just as the Tile Club members had tramped through East Hampton nearly 100 years before, "the place was now crawling with 'crazy' artists."

While much was gained by the postwar growth, much was lost, as well. In 1949, one of East Hampton's great homes, the Fens, was unexpectedly razed and the magnificent estate carved up into small lots. Soon, 250 acres in the town of East Hampton became home to 450 ranch houses. Not surprisingly, a New York magazine reported in the early 1950s, "The Ladies Village Improvement Society is adither with the menace of the ranch-house and summer-cubicle colonies advancing on both sides."

The *East Hampton Star*, once the East End's biggest promoter of progress, had come full circle, warning in September 1954, "Budget Headaches for Town Board as East Hampton Grows. More People Here; More Public Work; More Planning Needed." The A & P, the first supermarket in the Hamptons, opened on Nugent Lane, and diagonal parking in the village came to an end, allowing four lanes of traffic to accommodate the rising tide of yet another generation of newcomers. "The implications are staggering," the *Star* concluded.

Even the most casual observer will recognize that the challenges now facing the Hamptons are astoundingly similar to those endured and survived by their parents and grandparents. Almost every generation from the 1640s to the present has joined the battle between progress and preservation, whispering among themselves that this special community has finally, irrevocably been lost. Yet, time and again, the Hamptons have been rediscovered and enjoyed again by the children and grandchildren of those lamenting their loss. Good and bad, whatever changes have been wrought on this "quaint, quiet [and] queer" spit of land, the Hamptons' brilliant mix of air and light and sea continues to allure. "East Hampton is not perfect," one longtime East Hampton resident asserted as the 1950s came to a close, "but it works."

A LONG ISLAND DUCK FARM NEAR SOUTHAMPTON, C. THE 1940S. (Eric Woodward Collection.)

THE BIG DUCK, C. 1945. At one time about 80 percent of the ducks grown in the United States came from Long Island, with Long Island duck touted on menus in the finest restaurants nationwide. In the early 20th century, more than 100 duck farms flourished here. By 1970, there were just over 25 left. Today, fewer than a half-dozen farms remain in operation, mainly because groundwater pollution has rendered duck production neither popular nor profitable. The Big Duck on old Highway 24 in Flanders, which used to be the main gateway to the Hamptons, is now a bittersweet historical landmark, symbolizing the once important role of the poultry industry to Long Island. (Eric Woodward Collection.)

GREETINGS FROM SOUTHAMPTON, C. 1950. Even though the year-round population of the East End towns had nearly doubled from about 28,000 in 1900 to 46,000 in 1950, there was a constancy to the beach and beach life that could not be disrupted by man or nature. The poet John Hall Wheelock, who spent nearly his entire 91 summers in East Hampton, penned "Afternoon: Amagansett Beach" in 1956 as an ode to the East End: "The broad beach/ Sea-wind and the sea's irregular rhythm/ Great dunes with their pale grass/ and on the beach/ Driftwood, tangle of bones, an occasional shell/ Now coarse, now carven and delicate—whorls of time/ Stranded in space, deaf ears listening/ To lost time, old oceanic secrets. . . ." Of course, the bathing suits had changed. (Southampton Historical Museum.)

HERB MCCARTHY'S BOWDEN SQUARE, SOUTHAMPTON, C. 1950. Opened on Memorial Day of 1936, Herb McCarthy's Bowden Square (Southampton's "liveliest bodega") was the "in" spot for generations. Herb McCarthy played host to many celebrities, including Babe Ruth and Heddy Lamar, Ginger Rogers and Gary Cooper, and the Henry Fords, not to mention the Duke and Duchess of Windsor and nearly all the Gabor sisters. McCarthy, the very definition of social extrovert, was known to greet a returning blue-blood matron with, "Hello, sister. What's your name this year?" In 1986, Sen. Daniel Patrick Moynihan toasted the host in honor of his "hangout's" 50th anniversary: "Herb McCarthy is as much an institution as Bowden Square itself." Not long after, one of McCarthy's longtime regulars chirped as she slipped out into the night, "Don't leave us—where would we go?" McCarthy retired in 1986; the restaurant bearing his name was shuttered several years later. (Southampton Historical Museum.)

MONTAUK HIGHWAY AT MONTAUK LIGHTHOUSE, C. 1950. Despite the traffic congestion engulfing Long Island in the 1950s, handsome vistas like these could readily be found. Jeannette Edwards Rattray, co-owner of the *East Hampton Star*, described East End life in mid-century: "Outwardly, at least, this community remains substantially unchanged. The newcomer soon becomes as strongly opposed to any drastic change in East Hampton's appearance as any twelfth-generation descendant of pioneers. . . . He adopts the ways of the old-timers. A passionate devotion to the ideal village—beautiful, quiet, simple, dignified, cherishing its honorable history—seems to develop almost simultaneously with the arrival of any new settler." Rattray's comments ring as true in this new century as they did 50 years ago. (Southampton Historical Museum.)

SHINNECOCK INLET, SOUTHAMPTON, C. 1985. "No lovelier stretch of country, none more pleasing to the eye of artist or poet, none more peaceful or poetically happy in its outward expression, or more varied and interesting in its contour and color, is to be found anywhere along our Eastern Coast," scribbled one of the Tile Club members in 1879. He did not know how true his words would remain today—that each generation venturing to the East End would, despite all the changes, forever be intoxicated by "the fresh, green beast of the new world," as F. Scott Fitzgerald once imagined eastern Long Island. (Southampton Historical Museum.)

A Short History of the Picture Postcard

Postcards give us a window into the past. Unlike academic studies of architectural history or dry compilations of facts and figures in textbooks, postcards display a wonderfully democratic and unselfconscious view of the world. That populist element extended to the card writers themselves. People from all walks of life posted these cards to their friends and relatives. More than just casual communication and handsome pictures, postcards provide us with a valuable visual history. Sent first in the late 19th century, picture postcards with short messages penned on the back quickly became a fad across America by early in the new century. Quality photographic images of cities and towns were lithographed on card stock in Germany and sent back to local retailers in the United States for sale. In many locales, among them the East End villages, picture postcards are often the sole or best photographic depictions we have from the early 20th century.

In 1900, postcards cost only a penny to send (that is where we get the term "penny postcard"), and sometimes cards that were mailed early in the morning were even delivered the same afternoon. This was when few people had telephones in their homes and Western Union telegraph messages were expensive. For many, the postcard served as an inexpensive way to communicate the mundane details of daily life. Card sending was as common then as e-mail is today for quick correspondence. Southampton and East Hampton postcards are found in abundance because the towns had both a stable year-round population and a busy resort population. Locals and visitors alike would purchase and send picture postcards featuring their favorite scenic view.

In my collection of more than 2,400 postcards, there are cards showing hundreds of different depictions of Southampton and East Hampton, from bird's-eye views of the village streets to individual shopkeeper windows, from crowded beach vistas to empty byways, from early horse-drawn buggies to rounded 1930s sedans. As in most towns, the basic civic institutions, such as the post office, the town hall,

SHINNECOCK INN, SOUTHAMPTON, C. 1907. Built in 1906, the Shinnecock Inn, with 30 guest rooms and several dining rooms, cost about $60,000 and lasted only one season. The inn was designed to lure a new breed of visitors: the automobile traveler, golfers (playing at the already famous Shinnecock Hills Golf Club), and the shooting crowd (duck and shore birds abounded in the nearby hills). In 1908, the entire inn burned to the ground. (Eric Woodward Collection.)

and the bank, are often pictured. We also find cultural institutions well represented, including the Parrish Art Museum, Rogers Memorial Library, and the Meadow Club in Southampton, and the Maidstone Club, Clinton Academy, and Guild Hall in East Hampton.

Southampton's Lake Agawam was a favorite subject of cards, as were the giant homes that sprouted around its perimeter. In East Hampton, the Town Pond and Home Sweet Home (the residence associated with East Hampton's poet John Howard Payne) are portrayed on postcards again and again. These cards also show us how streetscapes and buildings changed from year to year: architectural fashions changed almost as fast as bathing suit styles.

Another special postcard heritage in the Hamptons is the large number of cards featuring estate homes. Many of the oversized cottages of the area were pictured on cards, often including the owner's name and the name of the house. Since most of these cards show the houses from the vantage point of the street, it seems likely that the owners did not encourage the commercialization of their own homes.

Postcard collectors, like all collectors, like to find rare and unusual examples. It is especially exciting to find an image of a building that no longer exists or was never documented except on one of these postcards. For example, in Southampton the large shingle-style Shinnecock Inn near the Shinnecock Golf Club burned down in 1907, one year after it was built. Only two postcards are among the surviving images of the building.

I am especially pleased that some of my postcards feature the towns' special events. The fairs in East Hampton, the founding-day pageants in Southampton, and other holidays and occasions were often commemorated on postcards. Just as compelling are the cards of shipwrecks and storms, although, surprisingly, I have seen none of the great hurricane of 1938, which almost blew the East End out to sea. In fact, just as we prefer our memories to accentuate the positive, the postcard view of life in the Hamptons and across the United States is generally sunny, well composed, and upbeat.

Of course, no fad lasts forever. By the start of World War I, the number of postcards published declined dramatically. With the novelty wearing off, the source for quality printing in Germany unavailable, and telephone service becoming increasingly inexpensive and convenient, their downfall was imminent. Fortunately, many postcards survived. We have three significant collections here on the East End: the Southampton Historical Museum Collection, the Harvey Ginsberg Collection at the East Hampton Library, and those in my own collection. I hope readers of *The Lost Hamptons* will enjoy the postcards reproduced in the book and the way of life they reveal as much as I have enjoyed collecting them for more than 20 years.

—Eric Woodward

ACKNOWLEDGMENTS

Richard Barons and I would like to thank the following individuals and institutions for their assistance in the making of this book.

Southampton Historical Museum: David Goddard, Sharen Dykeman, Hilary Herrick Woodward, and the Trustees;

East Hampton Library: Diana Dayton, Dorothy King, Michele Alison, Harvey Ginsberg (for his donation to the library), and the Board;

The Pollock-Krasner House and Study Center: Helen A. Harrison;

Sherrill Foster, Robert Hefner, and Mary Cummings;

Arcadia Publishing: Pam O'Neil and Brendan Cornwell.

I am also grateful to the following friends and colleagues who helped me—in so many ways—to complete this book.

Eric Woodward, a zealot in the best sense of the word, who so generously gave of his time, erudition, and collection to this project;

Ron Kraft, whose strength as an editor is surpassed only by the breadth of his knowledge; I have said it before and shall again: Ron edits the old-fashioned way, as a collaborator, teacher, and friend;

Richard Barons, my co-writer, whose steadfast energy, buoyant spirit, and meticulous attention to detail added so much to this book;

Richard S. Pine, my agent, who pushes me to grow, take risks—and dream;

Margot and Richard Petrow, my parents, for their love and support;

Jodi Paige-Lee, who brilliantly designed the original proposal and brought my concept into life—and living color;

Laura Ann Freeman, whose friendship and belief in me are unparalleled. *Namaste.*

Many thanks also go to Holly Atkinson, Susan Jessica Barnes, Larry Diamond, Paul Di Donato, Vince Errico, Julie Fenster, Joe Fox, Eduardo Garza, Denise Kessler, Brenda Laribee, Lora Ma-Fukuda, Cynthia Perry, Jay Petrow and Nancy Clarke, Julie and Maddy Petrow-Cohen, Susan Piver, Fred Silverman and Gerard Buulong, Peter L. Stein, Barry Raine, David Shiver, Mai Shiver, Robin Stevens, Pamela Strother, and Ellen Ullman.

ABOUT THE AUTHORS

STEVEN PETROW is an award-winning historian and journalist, with degrees in 20th-century American history from the University of California, Berkeley, and Duke University. Until recently, he was executive editor at Time Inc. A prolific writer, he has had works published in *Life Magazine*, the *Los Angeles Times*, and Salon.com. He is the author of four books, including *Dancing Against the Darkness: The Stories of People with AIDS, Their Families, Friends and Communities*. Petrow has received awards from the National Endowment for the Humanities and the Smithsonian Institution. He lives in Berkeley, California, but spends as much time as he can on Long Island's East End.

RICHARD BARONS is a native New Yorker who grew up in the Rochester area and currently lives in East Hampton. Educated at the State University of New York at New Paltz, he earned his undergraduate degree in art and architectural history, and he has worked in the fields of preservation and education ever since. He is currently director of the Southampton Historical Museum and was previously a curator at the Genesee Country Museum and at the Roberson Museum in Binghamton. Barons has consulted with many institutions, including the Henry Francis duPont Winterthur Museum, American Museum of Folk Art, and Old Sturbridge Village.

ABOUT THE CONTRIBUTORS

HELEN A. HARRISON is director of the Pollock-Krasner House and Study Center in East Hampton and is an art reviewer and feature writer for the Long Island section of the *New York Times*. Her latest book, *Hamptons Bohemia: Two Centuries of Artists and Writers on the Beach*, co-authored with Constance Ayers Denne, was published by Chronicle Books in 2002. She lives with her husband, the painter Roy Nicholson, in Sag Harbor.

ERIC WOODWARD is an architect registered in New York State and proprietor of his own four-man firm. He graduated in 1976 from Syracuse University with a bachelor of architecture degree. From 1980 to 1987, he was an architect with E.L. Futterman in Bridgehampton. He continues to be strongly involved with the Southampton Historical Museum, having been president of the Board of Trustees in the early 1990s. He is especially well known for his homes designed in the resort tradition of eastern Long Island and for his extensive collection of Hamptons and architectural postcards.